An opening

Born in Melbourne, Stephanie Radok has worked in Adelaide as an artist, freelance visual art writer and editor since 1988. She first exhibited her art at the Experimental Art Foundation in Adelaide in 1977 and her writing about art was first published in *Unreal City* in Canberra in 1986.

Stephanie Radok has a reputation as one of Australia's most lucid, fearless and best respected art writers, with over twenty years of extensive reviewing and critical writing for *The Adelaide Review*, *Artlink*, *Art Monthly* and other magazines. She has written many catalogue essays and was awarded a major New Work grant by the Australia Council in 2002. She was a Visiting Fellow in 2001 at the Centre for Cross-Cultural Research at the Australian National University. Over the last twenty years she has edited many issues of *Artlink* magazine discovering and encouraging new writers and artists and in 2011 co-edited the new series Artlink Indigenous breaking new ground in the appreciation of Aboriginal art in Australia.

As an artist, Stephanie Radok trained in Canberra and has exhibited widely. Her work has been collected by the National Gallery of Canberra, the National Gallery of Victoria, Flinders University Art Museum and private collections. Her art practice includes painting, printmaking, objects and installation. She has shown her work at Greenaway Art Gallery, the Art Gallery of South Australia, the National Gallery of Victoria, the Adelaide Festival Centre, the South Australian Museum, the Royal Adelaide Showgrounds and the Museum of Economic Botany. In 2011 a survey exhibition of her artwork The Sublingual Museum was shown at Flinders University City Gallery.

Also by Stephanie Radok
(with Dick Richards and Julie Blyfield)

Julie Blyfield

An opening

twelve love stories about art

STEPHANIE RADOK

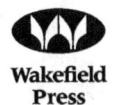
Wakefield Press

Wakefield Press
16 Rose Street
Mile End
South Australia 5031
www.wakefieldpress.com.au

First published 2012
Reprinted 2012, 2019

Copyright © Stephanie Radok, 2012

All rights reserved. This book is copyright. Apart from any
fair dealing for the purposes of private study, research,
criticism or review, as permitted under the Copyright Act,
no part may be reproduced without written permission.
Enquiries should be addressed to the publisher.

Typeset by Wakefield Press

National Library of Australia Cataloguing-in-Publication entry

Author:	Radok, Stephanie.
Title:	An opening: twelve love stories about art / Stephanie Radok.
ISBN:	978 1 74305 041 5 (pbk.).
Subjects:	Art in literature.
Dewey Number:	831.912

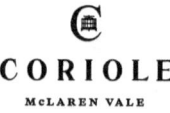 Wakefield Press thanks Coriole Vineyards for continued support

Contents

Preface		ix
Introduction		1
JANUARY	*the dignity of objects*	10
FEBRUARY	*the presence of the garden*	17
MARCH	*he is my relative*	23
APRIL	*finding water*	36
MAY	*the place of the dead*	43
JUNE	*a leaf from my book*	52
JULY	*measuring the world*	62
AUGUST	*a new language*	81
SEPTEMBER	*written on the skin*	103
OCTOBER	*reconstituting the ordinary*	116
NOVEMBER	*heart country*	128
DECEMBER	*the drawing of correspondences*	147
References		161
Index		169

for Jerome

There is a discourse about the arts, rarely written and at times unspoken which is neither that of historians so deeply tied to time and space nor that of critics concentrating on personal views about the arts ... It is a discourse of sensibilities affected by the excitement of visual impressions. It is the discourse of love.

Oleg Grabar

Preface

When we are young we live in no-time and all-time, when we get older we see that we are located in a specific time though we may not adopt the easy division of our lives into the decades and categories that are so smoothly described in newspapers and magazines. There is no dress rehearsal, no practice, no repeat performance, often no warning about the end of the show, so why do we store up experience, try to collect parts of our lives into patterns and examine them if not to learn something from them that we can use? We are made from memories of weather, pieces of paper and cloth, vegetables, fruit, days and moments strung together across blood, sinew and bone. Maybe some of us are made quite simply from the earth of one place, we taste strongly of one thing and belong to it. But most of us are made from many substances. We tend often to sum others up by their national or gender or racial or age or shape characteristics, yet truly each of us is a complex piece of embroidered cloth with different types of stitching and beading and threads and patterns and fringes, with a back and a front and an in-between. Or even a piece of cloth so full of holes that the background is also a part of us. And sometimes, someone or something reaches through the holes.

Like people art is made of complex patterns. The use we make of art depends on how we come across it in our lives – if it is around us everyday it can be especially transforming. It is an ordinary thing to buy or be given a calendar of twelve images to accompany the year. There is always something enthralling about a calendar – because it is not as precious as a book it can be dismantled without a sense of desecration, yet the images are in the format of a book, a closed object that opens up and contains

AN OPENING

revelations that can't be seen from the outside. We live with each calendar image for a month, it hangs on the wall marking the days of the week, the passage of time, both routine and special days, and observes us as we observe it, in good moods and bad, in tears or in laughter, celebration and commiseration. The month begins blank and then is filled with reminders and appointments. The image hangs calmly above all the days.

The power of an image or object to give comfort and thus somehow to give love is most mysterious and perhaps a certain amount of loneliness or at least solitude is required to really sense it. When we are reflected in the loving eyes of another person we may not see our more quiet reflection in a picture on the wall but on the other hand there is much loneliness and solitude within human relationships. The German artist Paula Modersohn-Becker, whose artwork is full of the weight of objects, the solid bodies of people, animals and flowers, and the palpability of light, expressed it thus:

I have cried a lot in my first year of marriage ... I feel as lonely as I did in my childhood ... It is my experience that marriage does not make one happier. It destroys the illusion that has been the essence of one's previous experience, that there existed something like a soulmate. The feeling of not being understood is heightened in marriage by the fact that one's entire life beforehand had the aim of finding a being who would understand one. But isn't it better to exist without such an illusion and look this great lonely truth straight in the eye.

And how does love get into or out of images? Is it the same as cooking, where love somehow gets in as part of the process of making and then emanates from the food and makes it good? Good food contains love; I know this to be true from experience because when I concentrate on making art my cooking goes awkward because the love has gone into the art. Of course

Preface

not every meal is made with overwhelming love, nor is every artwork. The ongoing popularity and appeal of Vincent van Gogh's work stems from the sense of love that emanates from his art; this is love in the form of the intense attention and energy he applied to his work, it is like electricity and can make your heart move in your chest. The question of how an emotion finds its way into a line, a shape, a colour or a substance, a piece of music or a movie, is deeply mysterious, but it does happen. There is no recipe for it but only a few works made by any person are truly full of it.

Images of artworks that I have torn or cut from calendars and attached to the wall over the years have had a great influence on me. In them I hang onto some deep reflective experience that they offer, these creations, these companions, some of which have accompanied me for years. Many are now lost but live on in my memory.

I remember a photograph of a sun-drenched small wooden jetty jutting into a lake surrounded by trees covered with summer-fresh green leaves and itself covered with reflections of leaves. The jetty was almost invisible in the light greens, the dark greens and the blackness of shadow. The photo was from a Russian calendar and was an archetypal Russian summer image; such fresh greens must be ephemeral and balanced by long months of cold and darkness. I remember a Paul Klee painting on coarse hessian in which a red balloon ascended through a sky of yellow triangles. A sense of simplicity, lightness, release, elevation and tranquillity shone out from the texture and colour of this image.

Another memorable one that I still have is a detail from Hieronymous Bosch's *The Garden of Earthly Delights*. A sense of wonder in this work, its colours, the proliferation of animals in it, has made it particularly precious to me. It has travelled from place to place and its edges are now tattered and discoloured. I once photocopied it at the local library with a lot of other images but somehow left it behind on the glass. When I got home and felt rather than saw the empty space on the wall and realised what I had done, I rushed back to ask for it, 'A picture of God with Adam and Eve in the Garden of Eden', and when they handed it over I saw it for a moment as what it was, a very ragged piece of paper, something they may have easily thrown away but which they must have been able to tell was valuable to someone.

Printed on this now worn but precious piece of paper is just part of the left-hand side of the triptych by El Bosco, as he is called in Spain, an artwork that hangs in the Prado in Madrid. This month, along with many other pilgrims, I finally saw the original. There were so many other visitors I was amazed as I thought my obsession with this work was private. What does everyone get from seeing these things, ticking off cultural treasures, touchstones, making them theirs? We've done that, goes the phrase: well, I've done the *Primavera*, and so on. And what do we do when finally we are there in front of the work we have gazed at in reproduction and dreamed of seeing in real life? Do we photograph it if we are allowed, do we memorise it inch by inch, go as close as possible to the surface of the work and try to see what can only be seen in the flesh? That's what I do, as well as making notes which gives me something to reread in order to re-visit the experience, to form my own idea of it from my own perception and, most urgently, to use the experience to create something of my own.

What we think are our private obsessions are not really private, or rather our private obsessions belong to many other people as well. Yet on this recent trip rather than being annoyed by the global nature of cultural tourism in the twenty-first century, the perennial crowds that make buying tickets on the

Preface

internet necessary, that mean queues to see certain works, that mean travelling in crowds, that even meant missing seeing things I wanted to see, I found it alright. It meant that as a solo traveller I was not completely alone but somehow part of a large anonymous family from many different countries who had travelled from our homes to see certain works of art. Thus the experience was solitary and individual but communal. Along with the works I could examine my fellow viewers and identify their languages and countries. How will each of us patch these sights into our lives, and are people really interested in art or mostly in fame or infamy? What does seeing artworks mean? Does viewing of contemporary art differ from viewing old art? What makes a work of art important, its place in history, its personal meaning, its financial value?

I was amazed to see the size of Bosch's painting (I had always imagined it to be tiny, a microscopic miracle, but it is as tall as me and much much wider). And I was enthralled to see the astonishing brightness of its colours – the reds, the yellows, the blues. What a miracle this painting must have seemed when it was first painted around 1500 and what a miracle it is now, Bosch's extraordinary imagination wedded to his skill, for the central image of the triptych is that amazing and endlessly fascinating *The Garden of Earthly Delights* of maybe five hundred playing naked male and female bodies, mostly white but some black, having adventures, couples standing on their heads next to giant owls, dancing and singing, or sailing along in giant berries rocked by lizards and so on in endless permutations, games and confabulations. The right-hand side of the triptych is *Hell*, a place of burning, humiliation, elaborate torture and pain. But the painting that I once collected from a calendar and have been looking at for many years, *The Creation of Eve*, the left-hand side of the triptych, is about neither pleasure nor pain but the peaceful heart of creation and the calm and curiosity of forms coming into being. Maybe after all I am one of the only ones for whom this least spectacular side of the painting is the most precious.

It is the contemplation of this painting that has given rise to this book as a place to pull together experiences and ideas, responses to art and the thoughts aroused by it, in order to partake of the miracle of creation and to add something to the world. The writing for each month begins with an artwork that is close to my heart. Many of them came to me as calendar pages, some as postcards, some in art galleries, others in books. As I wrote about them resonances kept cropping up — rivers that escape their beds, the colour yellow, birds — this seems to confirm some consistency in my thinking though I would not go so far as to call it a theory, more a calling.

Typically art exhibitions begin with an opening, a social event at which free drinks are served and friends come to congratulate the artist. The potential in every art exhibition, every artwork, is present at this point of opening, a point of potential expansion of the world, of surprise, celebration, learning and illumination. In taking *An opening* as the title for this book I wish to refer both to all the openings at which art is introduced to its audience, and to the bright clear light that characterises Australia which can be seen as potentially leading to an opening of the mind.

Introduction

At the beginning of his book *Modern Asian Art* about modernism in contemporary Asian art as neither a reflection nor a second-hand version of European art but a movement in its own right, John Clark quotes C.P. Cavafy's poem *Waiting for the Barbarians* in which the Greek poet asks: 'What will become of us without barbarians?' and answers: 'They were a kind of solution.' In his own words Clark describes the current opening up of the world through the changing of historical hierarchies thus: 'Byzantium is gone and the lands beyond it and the lands beyond them. We now begin to see each other, and no longer only the figments of force or imagination.'

The city of Byzantium stood at the geographical and cultural centre of the European and Middle Eastern worlds for more than one thousand years. It has long been used as a symbol of complexity and sophistication in art as well as an exemplar of cross-cultural fertilisation. In his poem *Sailing to Byzantium* W.B. Yeats described its essence as the song of a finely crafted gold and enamel bird. German artist Anselm Kiefer discussed the idea of Byzantium in *Boundaries, tracks, traces, songs*, a talk he gave in 1999 in Adelaide. The talk was illustrated by a single projected image of his 1989 painting *Abendland (Twilight of the West)* in which an embossing of a manhole cover represents the sun which sinks in a sky made of an immense battered sheet of lead. Beneath this literally heavy sky a ravaged whitened and scorched land surrounds a central image of receding train tracks and somehow we know that these tracks lead to Auschwitz, that the train has gone and that more trains will come, and that the tracks can never be erased and that the earth is scarred with the memory of such eternally recurring tragedies, akin to the time when Demeter lost Persephone to the underworld and the ensuing winter turned the earth white.

Kiefer's talk was filled with a brooding *Weltschmerz* of nostalgia and longing. He contrasted Western culture to Aboriginal culture which 'knows how to sing the land'. Strongly informed by the interpretations of Aboriginal culture he found in Bruce Chatwin's 1987 book *The Songlines*, Kiefer poetically mourned the decline of the West. Looking for a reference in his experience for Aboriginal dot paintings he compared them to Byzantine mosaics but queried the fate in them of the characteristic Byzantine sky that represents infinity and is typically composed of gold foil beneath clear glass. He asks:

> *But where is the sky, the golden background sky?...*
> *Coming from the Occident,*
> *From an ever sinking world,*
> *We do not have (the vault of) a golden sky above us any longer.*
> *And we never know how to re-create the land.*

I think there is a mistranslation in this last line and that Kiefer meant not 'know' but 'knew'; thus he means to say 'we never knew how to re-create the land' a version of the idea that Europeans destroy the land while indigenous people create or re-create it. The elegiac tone of Kiefer's words is typical of many self-accusatory Western voices. This self-disparagement ignores the richness and strength of Western culture, its admittedly

Introduction

sometimes ambivalent achievements, its long history of creativity and diversity, its strong connections to other cultures and its perennial potential for reinvention, rearrangement and rejuvenation; and indeed the recurring syncretism of all cultures. In answer to Kiefer's question about Aboriginal dot paintings — *where is the sky? where is infinity?* — as many such paintings are aerial views of the land made by people who spend much time reading tracks on the ground, it is possible to declare that both the artist and the viewers *are* the sky, or at least in the position of the sky. The infinite gold is in us, in our understanding or gathering of knowledge, the relationships and life we develop when we use it. We *are* the sky. Think of the fairy story in which the three sons dig the field looking for treasure; the outcome they discover is that the digging is the reward.

This book brings together some artworks that remain in my memory and continue to stimulate my ideas. It is what artworks make people feel or think that is important, not how much they cost or even who made them. Yet art is never placeless or timeless. The last twenty or so years in Australia, during which I have been both making art and writing about it, is the significant time in which Aboriginal art has blossomed in new ways. I have lived through this development, thought and written about it a lot, as well as about art made by non-Aboriginal people. I discern three main ways people have responded to Aboriginal art — ethnographically, formally and with rapture. The first concerns itself with stories and context, the second with abstract qualities while the third is haptic, visceral, emotional and ultimately about love.

Mine is not the interpreter or translator's voice that explains what the work means to the artists or takes the authoritative position of telling true inside stories. For every art story in the world there is always more than one true story anyway, and always many untold ones. A frequent approach to Aboriginal art is to see it as always needing translation by experts; this has had the effect of segregating it from other art. I believe Aboriginal art needs to be interpreted as more than illustrated stories, more than a cash crop or beautiful commodity for generating income and exemplifying national identity, and more than a functional component towards the social cohesion of indigenous societies in Australia, important though they all are. Aboriginal art is not timeless but exists in history and tells us a timely historical tale of survival and of conviction that the earth is sentient. What can be usefully learned from Aboriginal art may not be intricate facts or religious revelations, or indeed the bearing of an inferiority complex of being less spiritual or less connected to singing the land into being, but rather something metaphysical connected to general principles and approaches to living. Such as the importance of a sense of humour, of living in the present, of practical observation skills and respect for your own stories and ancestors whoever they are and however you find them; thus it may mean seeing art itself anew as always potentially a vital medium of human communication (rather than about fashion or investment or progress), as a source of connection to the world as well as a bearer of the conscious recognition of sharing the world with other life forms, animate and inanimate, past and present.

Like many other people my experience of indigenous people began very early in my life. First at primary school in America where the indigenous people were all called Indians, there was the concept of the Indian giver, and then there was the Indian burn (place two hands firmly around someone's arm and twist one hand one way and the other the other way – some people know this as a Chinese burn). Then there were the two trips my family made back and forth across America in the fifties on one of which we went through Colorado and the Mesa Verde

Introduction

National Park where we saw the extraordinary cliff dwellings and mesa-top villages with their windows cut into the earth, built between A.D. 450 and 1300 by the Pueblo Indians. And my older sister was given a book called *Indians and the Wild West: The story of the First Americans* which had a picture of an Indian on a horse on its cover. It was an especially shiny book and the Indian had a very shiny shaved head painted red and I was really scared of it and would carefully turn the book face down if I was in the room with it. It seemed very powerful. I had heard that the Indians scalped people and wasn't sure whether you bled to death after being scalped or not. Was that why his head was red? Maybe the Indian could come out of the photo and scalp you, he looked so shiny and alive. It made me breathless to think about it. Then there was the story all American children learnt at primary school about Pocahontas, daughter of Powhatan, saving the life of John Smith. No-one I knew spoke of present-day Indians so they seemed to be extinct, but they were certainly very present in stories.

In 1967 there was a referendum in Australia in which Aboriginal people gained the right to vote, to be citizens in their own country. I was at school in Adelaide and our class had a debate about the referendum, whether Aborigines should be allowed to vote. I was on the affirmative side and found no problem in saying simply that as democracy was about universal suffrage and the Aborigines were people therefore they should be allowed to vote, how could it be otherwise? The opposition said 'But they were a lot of "boongs".' I asked, 'What is this word "boong"'? The teacher was thrilled with this response, which I must admit was genuine ignorance rather than skill at debating, and I learned a little bit about racism.

In 1970 I saw for the first time my favourite film for many years, *Little Big Man* with Dustin Hoffman, fresh from his success

AN OPENING

and notoriety in *The Graduate*, playing a 121-year-old man telling his life story. I still remember the old Indian grandfather, played by Chief Dan George, making a point of saying, every day of his life, 'Today is a good day to die' (I still sometimes say it to myself); that Cheyenne means Human Beings; that everything in the world is alive; and Hoffman's character saying in his high-pitched whiny 121-year-old voice: 'Pawnees was always sucking up to Whites.' Thus pointing out I guess that all Indians are not the same. In my final year of secondary school, in my editorial for the school magazine in a mood of anti-materialism and counter-cultural fervour I quoted approvingly from Henry David Thoreau's *Walden* about the Muclasse Indians who burn all their goods at the end of each year.

What I am concerned to emphasise is the need to value art as an experience rather than an investment or an illustration. A significant thread in the following pages in the stories about me, love and art, is the renewal and survival of indigenous cultures. The presence amongst us of the first peoples of the earth, not extinct, not superseded, not mere legends or myths but here and now, is miraculous and worth dwelling on.

How do you know who your people are? Is identity always tied back to the past, to history, birthplace, blood, ethnicity and nationality, or can it also be bigger than all those things and be found or discovered in the present, or invented, like some traditions? Does being here in this suburb before my neighbour give me more rights? If I came to Australia from somewhere else does it mean I can never belong? If I have a small family or no family does it make me less important, or if I don't know the deep history of my family does it make me worthless? What if I have to run away from my family? Can I look outside family for kinship? Historian and activist Marcia Langton wrote:

Introduction

The impetus for Australians to value Aboriginal culture might arise from a sense of this culture as being a part of their own heritage and their own historical legacy, not just that of exoticised and demonised others.

An intuition about dot paintings as showing an earth that mirrors the sky came to me forcefully in Clifford Possum's retrospective exhibition in 2003. Possum's paintings involve a complex layering of imagery, but his friend, writer and historian Vivien Johnson told me in conversation that when she said that he must have a good brain to be able to see a whole work in his mind's eye before painting it, he said: 'Not brain but heart.' His five large extraordinary map paintings, *Warlugulong* made with Tim Leura (1976) and the solo works *Warlugulong* (1977), *Kerrinyarra* (1977), *Mt Denison Country* (1978) and *Yuutjutiyungu* (1979), were all shown in one gallery space; four were hung vertically and one was horizontal in the middle of the space on a low platform. Of course each was painted flat on the ground. These extraordinary and beautifully detailed paintings of the topography of Possum's country, and the incidents from multiple Dreaming stories belonging to it, can be studied with their accompanying diagrams which were recorded by art adviser John Kean when they were painted. The diagrams translate every shape and mark, except what may be secret, thus demonstrating this pictorial language as something that can be read like a book, full of story and incident, description and insight. To learn it is like learning hieroglyphics or pictograms. Here the ancestors travelled over the land creating its features; here they taught a ceremony or performed it for the first time; here they ate or had a fire; here they hunted, camped, danced or were transformed. It is a way of remembering a landscape, a mnemonic for a place and many other things connected to it. Yet at the same time another, perhaps equally rich, way to experience these paintings is to visually wander through them just like our eyes wander through the stars in the night sky, from depth to surface, from near to far, from pattern to spaciousness, from easily interpretable story-trace and familiarity to the unknown. To know that they are meaningful, that their marks are full of purpose, but to hang back from learning their language, to remain in an unknown place, to experience delight and mystery without striving for facts or interpretation and to appreciate the sense of space that they possess, the patterns and textures and the colour relationships that they show – pink against brown, yellow with white, red ochre on black, especially the glowing yellow – can be a very satisfying and rapturous state. I see them as star maps that you can feel inside you. They embrace infinity and wonder by recreating the experience of looking at the night sky and drawing attention to our co-existence in the sky with the stars. After I was thinking about them I had an incredibly vivid dream in which the earth literally slid up to the sky which was covered with multiple, slowly spinning mosaics made of stars. And I knew then that it was possible to know the sky as you might know a house or a garden, and that you might then also think of the sky as a mirror to the earth and the earth as if it was water reflecting the sky.

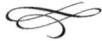

At this point of writing I went outside where, in early May, the leaves of the nectarine tree are slowly turning from green into a luminous glowing orangey yellow, a colour so rich and pure it can barely be described. To collect a leaf I only need to touch it, as they are ready to fall and indeed several are scattered on the ground near the recently planted broad beans which are starting to throw their strong, broad, bright green leaves into the air. The

Introduction

nectarine leaf is smooth and perfect, a folded curved half-moon of colour. From the central vein along its fold other veins branch out, making up the pattern of its circulation. Its edges are very finely serrated; its stem is tinged with pink. I know that if I press it in a book it will keep its colour for many years. When I look closely at it I feel some memory stirring within me, a memory that connects me to myself as a child first discovering the world, first responding to it, first getting to know shapes and colours and forms by looking very closely at things, and somehow both going inside them and putting them inside me.

JANUARY
the dignity of objects

Pebbles cannot be tamed
to the end they will look at us
with a calm and very clear eye

Zbigniew Herbert

In 1960 when I was six I spent the day in the National Gallery of Art in Washington with my mother and sister. At the end of the day for being 'good' I was allowed to choose a print from the gallery shop. The print I chose was *Still Life*, painted in 1866 by Henri Fantin-Latour. It possesses the quiet bright presence of most still lives. Such works are not all the same, but all possess a sense of the implacability of objects, their calmness or sense of moral certainty. I remember that choosing it was an act bearing in mind my older sister who had been 'bad' and complained that she was hungry most of the day. Did we really spend a day there? More likely it was a morning or an afternoon, two hours that felt like four to her. Because the painting has food in it I had the idea that it was for my sister as well as for me. I didn't want to be singled out as the 'good' one and have to face either her misery or her revenge. I am surprised at this memory but I guess I was, for the sake of peace, always thinking I could calm everyone down.

January

Our family's agitation seemed to have no end, though on reflection it was mostly emanating from the endless restless exhausting energy exuded by my father which I got to experience spasmodically again in later life, though never to understand or to feel calm about being anywhere near him, except perhaps when he was dying. As I stood next to his bed in a public hospital, in the steamy heat of Bangkok where he had lived for the previous twenty years, shocked by the clear imminence of death in his shattered body, he made faces at me and tried to get up and go home (this chronic impatience was partly the reason that his stitches were torn and complications set in). Did he know that he was so close to death? Maybe, though he certainly planned to live longer, had things to do and was, after all, only eighty-four. Perhaps he knew because, most unusually, he asked me to kiss him before I left. It was also at this time that his Thai wife and I both saw his hands next to mine on the bedclothes and saw they were practically identical (though mine are smaller) – 'same, same' we said to each other. How strange I had never noticed this before.

What can you ever say to a practically deaf man who never wanted to hear anything he didn't want to hear? When you are a child it means that you learn to be silent. He was unable to relax or let people be, though would occasionally collapse onto a sofa for an hour or so in the early evening, at which time a tiny bit of peace would descend on our home. Of course he did go to work and travel, and at such times rather than spend time together the three of us would each look for and find the simple peace of solitude as a way of regenerating. Thus at dinner, though we would sit together, each of us would read a book or sometimes watch TV but rarely talk. When he was there we were on guard throughout the meal which often – actually almost always – ended in tears or slamming doors. Being both predictable and unpredictable it created surges of emotion that ruined my digestion. My sister used to always loyally take my mother's side while I, displaying the odd ability to see two sides of an argument, tried to find some kind of rationale in each parent's words as they maddened and goaded each other. When he finally left home for good in 1968, a few months before the Russians invaded Czechoslovakia, our relief was immense, though he continued to the end of his life to apologise for going. I was never able to tell him how very glad we all were.

Yet he could be generous, kind and charming, and was a good cook, highly intelligent and hard-working. Born to a Jewish father and German mother in 1920 in East Prussia, he had escaped alone from Germany in 1939 and met up with two of his older brothers in England. The three of them were interned as 'enemy aliens' when war broke out and put on a ship, the *Arandora Star*, for Canada, which was torpedoed, then finally sent to Australia on the *Dunera*, on which the European internees were notoriously treated inhumanely by the British crew. Arrival in Australia meant further internment at Hay and then at Tatura Internment Camp, a place where grateful peace from the war raging in Europe was connected with fear for those left behind as well as astonishment at the climate, flora, fauna and people of this strange land they had arrived in. Among the prisoners, who ranged widely in age and experience, were many German–Jewish intellectuals, so a university was set up and the primitive art expert Leonhard Adams was made pro-rector. A famous linocut called *Desolation, Internment Camp, Hay NSW* by another prisoner, artist Ludwig Hirschfeld Mack, shows a solitary figure standing behind barbed wire gazing up at the Southern Cross.

In later years someone who loved my father described him to me as a hamster always trying to escape. He would rush out of cinemas if the film bored him. In a museum he would gallop through all the galleries and be ready to go in five minutes. If you managed to stand up to him and stay to look he would hurry off and go for a long rapid walk before returning to collect the stragglers with impatient comments. Everything was a rush, thus everything became an emergency. He was also always making profound all-encompassing statements about Life, maybe a German trait of thought which I have inherited along with the hands.

The Fantin-Latour *Still Life* painting on the other hand reflected something of the spirit of my half-Irish, part Scottish and part British rather irreverent red-headed Australian mother, her amateur but devoted empathy for literature and art, and her embrace of idleness bordering on laziness. She grew up in both Melbourne and the Mallee, and studied journalism at the University of Melbourne in the 1930s but left to work for an insurance company when her stepfather died. She was the one who enjoyed looking at pictures with me and perhaps introduced me to it as an escape from family tension. She collected books and vases, gardened, and enjoyed smoking and drinking more than eating. Picking flowers and arranging them in the right vase to create a picture, a moment of beauty, was an abiding pleasure for her.

The painting shows a book, a vase of pink and white camellias, a black and red lacquered Japanese tray, a half-peeled mandarin, a basket of fruit including quinces, apples and pears, and a fine white porcelain teacup and saucer with a gold rim. The painting includes just one teacup, because this is not a tea party but an image of pleasurable solitude involving food, drink and intellectual sustenance. The novel is a French one with a plain blue cover.

Fantin-Latour, who painted between 1856 and 1904, is best known for his flower paintings and still lives from which he made a living, though he sold most of them in England not in France where he lived. He also painted four notable group portrait scenes of his friends Manet, Whistler, Rimbaud, Verlaine, Baudelaire, Renoir, Zola, Monet and other less well-known artists and writers. Surely the sensitivity with which Fantin-Latour painted the lips of the young Rimbaud and the eyes of Verlaine in the 1872 painting called *A Corner of the Table* are the same skills he used on the surfaces of teacups and flowers.

I have often enjoyed the kind of tea party for one implied in my Fantin-Latour print by coming home from the library with a stack of new books, arranging tea and a plate of fruit, then feeding from them all for a few hours, sipping tea, peeling and slicing fruit, dipping into the books here and there, dog-earing the corners of certain pages or more respectfully slipping in torn strips of paper or bookmarks, devouring the words, the ideas, the images, occasionally looking up to stare out of the window, into the sky or the trees and travelling still further in thought. What am I searching for? A few fragments of common feeling, ideas, information about art, about history, about cultures and the making of objects and thoughts, fitting pieces together, the description of something that I have also thought or felt, a feeling of contact, revelation, enlightenment, epiphany. I feed this enjoyment by copying down sentences, noting pages, building and locating an ancestry, a web of connections. To find a voice that takes me confidentially inside another person, the miracle of someone writing in another place and time, sometimes in another language, and speaking through that writing inside my head with a detail and sensitivity rarely expressed by anyone I meet, or to see in an artwork something of the heart of another person, are precious experiences that make me feel alive, that I search for to keep me alive.

In the Fantin-Latour still life the palpability of the objects, the sense that they have been and will be touched is very important. Like the fat novel covered in blue paper the pears are heavy, like

January

the red and black lacquer tray the apples are smooth and shiny, the quinces are downy, the mandarin has soft white fluff inside its skin and on the outside that typical pitted citrus texture full of tiny pores of oil which can be squeezed to get an intense scent. The camellias in their shiny blue glass vase have soft petals like flesh that can be marked with a fingernail, yet they also possess the perfection of porcelain. In a minute an entire flower may simply drop off its stem without a sound. It is an artwork that seems ordinary and slight yet is tenderly about texture and weight, both physical and emotional. The peaceful halls of the National Gallery in Washington, walking through them looking at pictures with my mother, trying to appease my sister with painted food, being quiet for my father, looking for my own place in words and images, are all there in the painting for me.

Still life art is often said to be about the love of possessions, or simply death. It is said that the transience of the perfection of fruit and flowers caught at the point of ripeness imitates our own fragile state of mortality, but to me still life evokes conversation with another person through a book, food or a work of art; and above all stillness, a quiet receptiveness, a moment seized from the constant movement of life, a space of contemplation in which the openness of a vessel is like an opening heart turned towards another one.

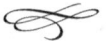

About once a week I take the dog to the park at the top of the street. As the bronze sign on the stone gatepost says, it was given to the people of Australia by Miss A.E. Ferguson in 1945 as a National Pleasure Resort. It is a type of bush called grey box woodland. You might call it scrub rather than bush. It is a dry scratchy place which once would have been thought of as wasteland waiting to be developed, turned into something real or useful. It is never watered. Today it is recognised as one of the best relict scrub reserves of the Adelaide Plains, a valuable reminder of the Black Forest that covered these foothills when Adelaide was first settled by Europeans in 1836. Even though this piece of land has never been farmed there are Cape lilies and soursobs, plantain and nasturtiums, weeds from South Africa, Europe and the rest of the world growing on it among the natives like grey box gum trees, clasping goodenias, orchids, sundews, native cherries and cranberries, wattles and delicate callitris pines. A representative few of the native plants have been signposted but most of them have resisted being made into a living museum and died, though the signs remain. Native cherry says a sign, while a few weeds stick their dry arms and legs up near the signs looking like, well, weeds. The park contains possums, lizards, butterflies, birds and sometimes koalas. One of the most noticeable things about it is its intense dryness compared to the watered green lawns associated with public spaces. The soil is a sandy grey powder and the vegetation has a petrified, stiff quality, as if becalmed or preserved beneath glass, held in the stillness of a silent enchantment. The paths through it are hard smooth compacted earth. Here and there in summer balls of honey-coloured resin shine out on the trunks of wattle trees.

FEBRUARY
the presence of the garden

Out of himself like a thread the child spins pain
and makes a net to catch the unknown world.
Judith Wright

In May 1961 we left North America and got on a ship to Europe. No one is alive now to tell me exactly how that decision was made, but I remember for our last meal we went to eat in Chinatown in New York with one of my father's students whose father was Japanese and worked at the United Nations with U Thant. At a grand dinner he gave all the ladies an original *ukiyo-e* woodblock print by Hiroshige. In earlier days it hung in our house in a room with a number of other Japanese prints removed from books and framed, including a very mesmeric one by Utamaro of a woman looking into a mirror where her face is seen only in the mirror. There were also objects from Japan brought back by my mother's family at the end of the war — two sets of fine wooden lacquer cocktail glasses — an orange-red set painted with gold images of irises, bamboo, wisteria, peony and cherry blossom and a black set with golden roosters. The black set had a matching cocktail shaker and a round tray. There was also a small ceramic teapot wrapped around with green leaves, butterflies, birds and pink flowers. These treasures were displayed upon an elegant glossy black free-standing dresser with drawers full of cloth napkins, candles, boxes of silver-plated cutlery including bone-handled fish knives and mother of pearl serving utensils, and shelves full of fragile glass and china behind sliding doors on one side and a low narrow shelf to display large books or magazines on the other side. It was called The Room Divider. Remembering these objects is like becoming aware of a scent rising out of an old drawer that brings back The Past even though what is actually being brought back is hard to grasp. It is not the evocative scent of flowers or perfume, it is more like the indefinable scent given off by the kind of old plastic that is no longer made, or the particular dust that collects on the metal of old slide projectors and cameras. It raises memories of being small and secret, hidden under tables or beds accompanied by miniature books and tableaux of toy animals.

The ambience of my childhood buried inside me is deeply attached to these images and objects. It was a place of instability and mystery where people and places moved but some objects were stable, where images in pictures on the wall provided serenity and sustenance, and art was both consolation and communion. As I write these words I look really closely and deeply at objects, artworks and images in books. Somehow this refreshes and transforms my eyes and thoughts to such an extent that when I enter our rather worn bathroom its old pink tiles glow fresh and luminously at me, and when I walk through the house all the surfaces, shadows and shapes surrounding me are transfigured to become more real, more gracious, more eloquent than at other times when they are an almost invisible shell around me.

In this old suburban house the presence of the garden is everywhere. Through open doorways and windows the outside comes in to be part of the inside, the eyes travel deep into trees, bushes and the spaces within them, the reflections on the wooden floor show the light reflecting off leaves, glowing shapes of sky and trees, stretched auras of light. The garden was not designed but grew. Its tangled harmony is like that of roses which no matter how carelessly you push them into a vase always fall into a beautiful arrangement.

I have a postcard of an interior painted in 1955 by Grace Cossington Smith stuck to the wall in the laundry above the old square white ceramic trough. At first the painting appears to show a window, but it is really a mirror on a wardrobe next to another wardrobe with a door opening onto shelves on which piles of folded clothes are stacked. The mirror door reflects yet another door that is open to the verandah and the garden beyond. The whole work contains a lot of yellow in broad square panes of paint, like pieces of solid light pouring in to flood the room with radiance and a kind of dissolving energy. The postcard is next to the laundry window that looks out onto two plum trees and an olive tree, but it is the tiny painting that suggests an escape from domesticity which is nevertheless embedded in the domestic, the possibility of glowing visions in a lump of butter or a drop of light like a coin on a window sill.

Our garden is a marvellous adventure, an untamed place, an anomaly amongst the overregulated gardens around us, a place to dream. There are parts of it where you can hide among bamboo and jasmine, where time is visible in overgrowth and undergrowth. There are miniature cities of succulents quietly growing into tiny empires, a two-metre high fennel clump, grape vines, untouched places of still dirt and silent stones, weeds that are herbs, herbs that grow like weeds, self-sown trees, piles of oyster shells, fig, apricot, quince, olive and plum trees, rocks from the quarry up the hill that have quartz crystals tucked into them, an old banksia tree we planted when my son was small, and sections where you can walk through head-high white daisy bushes in spring.

Hung in the cool darkness of the house the Hiroshige *ukiyo-e* print is Number 81 from his *One Hundred Famous Views of Edo*. Made in the fourth month of 1857 its title is *Ushimachi, Takanawa*, the name of a place on the southern edge of Edo (now Tokyo). *Ukiyo-e* is always translated as pictures of the floating world, the world in which we live – evanescent, fragile, glowing. The image shows a sea and a sky with the classic Japanese woodblock fade dropping in the sea from white at the horizon to light blue to deep blue and rising in the sky from pink near the horizon to white to pale blue to dark grey at the top. These fades create the illusion of depth and space, as well as of moistness in the air. It is a scene on a dock at dawn, the pink in the far horizon shows the beginning of the day. The position of the viewer is that of a child or a dog, lying under and behind the wooden wheel of a large wagon in the shade. A section of the wheel, its spokes and rim, fills the right front of the image. The sea is filled with sailing boats, moored or leaving the harbour, while others are out at a distant headland or on the horizon. The work seizes a fragment of time, a very ordinary moment in an ordinary place. There are two spotted pig-like dogs standing near the wagon, one of them holds a piece of string with a worn-out straw sandal on the end of it, a traditional symbol for the end of a journey, and near them two pieces of chewed watermelon rind on the ground mark the season as summer. As in a haiku, place, season and time of day are marked simply and subtly in this quiet image that is a lot like one of those accidental oblique photos that you take when you are unpacking your camera.

February

The *One Hundred Famous Views of Edo* series was Hiroshige's last work completed just before his death in 1858 at sixty-two. It was celebrated in Japan and influenced the Impressionists, especially Vincent van Gogh, who made oil studies of two of the prints. Our Hiroshige print makes me think of silent dinners and watchfulness. It holds some of my secret history and many memories of our family journey from America to Europe in the fifties, from Europe to Australia in the sixties, of our new favourite toy, the Etch A Sketch, sitting in the back window of the car as it disappeared into the ship's hold (we never saw it again), of our American clothes somehow also lost in the hold of the ship, of our strange new clothes bought in port or on the ship, and the loss of almost everything else familiar twice in a few years. The print seems to remember the deracination, the resilience, the fragments that people hold onto, the way lines can both curve and lie flat on paper and how a colour can be a place of belonging or of love ...

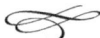

Today the dog and I walk out early in a faint white mist of scented transpiration from the land after dawn. It has been hot for days and will be hot for many days to come. When we find a fallen tree branch he insists on stopping and examining the leaves and twigs so closely I always think he believes there is a piece of the sky caught in it. All the patchy-skinned gum trees we pass, big and small, seem to have exploded in the heat from the amount of bark lying beneath them, and the smooth lemon-scented gums have also stripped off their pink bark and stand looking newly naked and greenish yellow. We see a crested pigeon fanning his tail up, fluffing his body out, lowering his head and dancing for another pigeon. Then the first pigeon dances for the second one. Every now and then I catch the faint scent of water on dirt. It reminds me of being a child crouching down to turn a stiff metal tap on a tank and fill a water bottle, while feeling myself bleached pale and as transparent as the water in the blazing heat and white light of an Australian summer.

MARCH

he is my relative

The Chamacocos of Latin America [who are descendants of ancient nomad hunters who are today mostly farmers and day labourers] listen to radios and tape recorders, walk to Bahía Negra to make phone calls and dream of having their own motorcycles. But when the night falls, they tell, whispering and staring at the fire, stories that took place before the beginning of time. Then at an invisible signal, they enter the jungle looking for their deepest identity, erase their faces with masks, cover themselves with paint, feathers and cries, shed their identities and become gods and strange birds.

Ticio Escobar

Pinned to the wall above my desk is a detail of the left panel from Hieronymous Bosch's *The Garden of Earthly Delights* triptych which hangs in the Prado in Madrid. I have been looking at this painting that I cut from a calendar since I was about twelve and it has always renewed in me a sense of wonder at the natural world, and the multiplicity and fertility of its creation. The stillness of it is a place for me to retreat and I always find some new detail or event in it.

The work has a solemn topic; God has just created Eve and is introducing her to Adam who has woken from the sleep that he was in while God got out his rib to form Eve. God is embodied as someone who looks like Jesus, a tall bearded man in long pink robes, holding Eve's wrist in his left hand and holding his right hand up in a blessing gesture. Adam sits on the ground, like an obedient child, his feet fidgeting a bit with the edge of God's robe. Eve is in a kneeling position but does not actually seem to connect with the ground. Adam looks across at her with interest, partly at her face, partly at her breasts. Her eyes are downcast. Behind Adam a tree draws the eye as much as the figures, but it is not an apple tree, it is a Dragon Tree. It is not, my book on Bosch tells me, the Tree of Knowledge but the Tree of Life.

There are many such trees around Adelaide. An entire row of them lives along King William Road flanking the western border of Government House. A magnificent specimen spreads over the flamingo enclosure at the zoo. A terrific one is now visible at the edge of the eastern parklands since a building was pulled down at the old Victoria Park racecourse. The Waite Arboretum has quite a few. Once you know what they look like you start to see them in private and public gardens all over the place, at least in Adelaide.

Dragon Trees are not strictly speaking trees but large succulents. They originally come from the Canary Islands, known to ancient European civilisations as The Fortunate Islands. The name *Islas Canarias* is said to be derived from the Latin term *Insula Canaria*, meaning Island of the Dogs. The original inhabitants of the island, the Guanches, used to worship dogs, mummified them and treated them generally as holy animals. The Islands were claimed by Portugal in 1341 and ceded to Spain in 1479, not long before Bosch painted this image. Located off the west coast of Morocco, the islands have fertile soil and a Mediterranean climate but central peaks high enough to carry snow all year. In 1492 Christopher Columbus used the Canary

Islands as the staging post for his first trip to America. The exact date that Bosch's painting was made is unknown, but around 1500 is the usual time given. Somehow a sense of the New World found over the sea has entered this painting. It is made with a strong sense of the restless and unpredictable nature of creation. For Old World peoples the finding of new forms of plant and animal life not mentioned in the Bible and the absence of archetypal plants like grape vines, figs and olive trees, called the entire creation of the world into question.

Dragon Trees (*Draceana draco*) get their name from their shape; their branches are like arms, each time they flower a new branching division is created leading to a many-armed and many-headed look. Their name also comes from their deep red sap, which is known as dragon's blood. The resin is exuded from the wounded trunk or branches of the tree. Ladon, the hundred-headed dragon which guarded the Golden Apples of the Hesperides (the nymph daughters of Atlas, the Titan who holds up the sky thus keeping it from embracing the earth), was killed by Hercules as his Eleventh Labour. The blood that fell became Dragon Trees. Another story of origin for Dragon Trees, told by Pliny, tells of the struggle between a dragon-like basilisk and an elephant that at its climax led to the mixing of the blood of both creatures. Pollen records indicate that twenty million years ago the trees stretched from the Canary Islands all the way to southern Russia.

A part of every witch's pantry, dragon's blood is a crimson resin highly prized since ancient times and said to have been used by the Egyptians in mummification processes. It appears in the Bible alongside frankincense and myrrh, and was used as a medicine, dye and as a fake stone in jewellery. On the island of Soqotra, the island of bliss, east of Africa in the Indian Ocean, where its very similar sister tree *Dracaena cinnabari* is a source of cinnabar, dragon's blood is used to this day for stomach problems, as furniture varnish, to dye wool, freshen the breath, decorate pottery and houses, and even as lipstick. Often carried on sailing boats for their medicinal properties, Dragon Trees were on William Dampier's ship when he landed on the west coast of Australia in 1674. He wrote that most of the trees that he saw were Dragon Trees on account of the colour and flavour of their sap. Dampier must have been referring to a bloodwood eucalypt or gum tree, because of its beads of red sap, and then imagined its long arms and straight leaves to be some antipodean modification of the Dragon Tree's thick trunk and limbs, and strap-like leaves.

Dragon Trees are miraculous trees, fabulous trees, trees with arms like human limbs that seem about to move. Their very strangeness suggests not mere growth but design. They intimate a plan for a tree rather than an organic form. Like a drawing or a dream, so strange and yet perfectly real, they look supernatural, legendary, mythic. The forms of other plants from the early days of life on earth, such as cycads, tree ferns and baobabs, in which function finds form in ways that are both direct and extravagant, are similarly bold. The strong simplicity of these forms is resonant and surely connects with some primal image bank within us. Their shapes join and divide with an enormous sense of rhythm, purpose, harmony and balance.

To see a thriving Dragon Tree in the clear light of Adelaide and to recognise it as the same as the Tree of Life painted by Hieronymous Bosch is both marvellous and surprising. However lateral an experience, it seems to mean more than the simple recognition of a transplanted tree, an immigrant, as it involves a link to a depiction of a creation story that celebrates the diversity of life and the excitement of its mutability. Although Bosch's painting was made in the Northern Hemisphere more than 500

March

years ago, it resonates today in the Southern Hemisphere with a strong implication of human interconnectedness across time and place. It suggests links between imagination and nature – and quite a lot of what Werner Herzog calls ecstatic truth – in inexplicably connecting to Australia.

Around the three figures of God, Eve and Adam in Bosch's painting there are animals of all sorts, many of which must have died in the Flood because they differ from all currently existing animals. Floating in the pond, a small creature with a bill like a duck is reading a tiny book. It seems to have a tail like a fish with which it balances itself but, apart from the tail, it looks just like a platypus, even though the work was painted about 300 years before platypuses were seen outside Australia. Then there is a dignified magpie standing casually near Adam in a magpie-on-alert kind of way, looking as if it is about to throw back its head to sing or slice across the sky and clip a dog in the ear. However, it doesn't look like a European Magpie at all, but like its distant relative the White-backed Australian Magpie, of the butcherbird family, native to South Australia, Central Australia and Victoria, and whose sweet warble or flute-like carolling is such a familiar part of the morning in these places. An early recorded vernacular name for it was Piping Roller, written on a painting of it by the Port Jackson Painter in Sydney sometime between 1788 and 1792.

This magpie is the third feature of Bosch's painting, beside the Dragon Tree and the near-platypus – that miraculously connect it to the Australia I live in. Almost like a code, each of them emphasises that the profundity of relationships between animals and people, trees and people, places and people, exquisitely present in this artwork, spans the globe, centuries and cultures.

In looking at the painting it is the idea of creation that is manifestly present, the idea of the world being formed from nothing, and the idea of purpose and intent. On top of the calm inevitability of creation there is the diversity, the plasticity of the world and the marvel of it all exuberantly expressed in such hybrid mutant wonders as unicorns and three-headed winged lizards. Above and beyond any religion or creator is the teeming energy of the world with its irrepressible and unpredictable metamorphoses.

Does the making of an artwork have any relationship to the creation of the world? Are we as humans able to have special understanding because we are both created and creators, playing the role of both artefacts and gods?

Indigenous cultures all over the world revolve around their creation stories. Their knowledge of creation and of the stories and acts, songs and dances connected with it embed them in circuits of certainty, and maintain their confidence about their relationships to the world around them. We might say that the purpose of knowing a creation story is to feel connected and confident, and that to feel confident and connected you need to know a creation story, evidence of which is in your vicinity. This certainty has been exchanged in many Western societies for scientific hypotheses in the care of experts. Clearly all people do come from and belong to the earth, but the stories of the many indigenous people all over the world suggest that they know which bit of the earth they come from and they can interpret it in terms of their own culture.

What does it mean to believe a creation story: that a tree grew from the blood of a dragon; that God made the world in six days; that the Wagilag Sisters and Wititj, the olive python, were responsible for the first monsoon as well as the first dances, songs and laws about marriage and ceremonies? How does it affect your relationship to the world; does it give you an enhanced sense of the preciousness of what is here and of your close connection to it; does it mean you have a concept of belonging, of sacredness, of holiness, of mystery that pervades your life in the form of knowledge, objects and acts that relate to a non-visible world within, behind and inside the visible? Is such a concept only received through cultural indoctrination, or can it be derived from intuition? Does it mean that you see connections and analogies between various phenomena? That you have an openness to finding qualities like feelings in trees, insights in animals, intuitions in plants; that you don't separate people from other living or non-living parts of the world but see them as of equal value, of equal standing, as truly somehow interchangeable? Can you invent your own creation story or feel it out or must it be handed down from generation to generation? What if the link is broken between generations? Is there a contemporary creation story that is credible or useful; what purpose would it serve?

Every creation story, whether it is about evolution, divinity or ancestors, posits the wonder and rightness of what happened, each contains the arbitrary in balance with the inevitable. Things turned out the way they did but it could have been different. There is something truly marvellous about this necessity and its related sense of contingency.

Evolution is a profound creation story that connects everything on and to the earth. Each time art is made it reflects or remakes part of the world. Art that draws our attention to the earth underlines the importance of the relationship between humans and nature. This is a literal relationship as all beings on the earth are related; our origins are the same. The shapes of plants, of animals, of landforms, of skyforms, have a resonance within us that is lodged in our eyes and brains at the most fundamental level. The correspondences between leaves and hands, trees and lungs, flowers and sex organs, affirm connection as well as transmutation.

AN OPENING

The affirmation of connectedness that lies within the recognition of these correspondences emphasises our corporeal being, or in simple terms 'it grounds us'. It is said that from one piece of your DNA it would be possible to re-create your entire body, so all of you is present in it, something like a convex mirror that holds a room in a circle of glass. It is also said we share eighty per cent of our DNA with trees. Our attachment to creation stories, whether literal, metaphoric or scientific, is also an attachment to our own creative and explanatory powers. DNA is characterised by beauty, elegance and randomness. Purpose and lack of purpose, meaningfulness and meaninglessness intermingle and exchange positions. Beauty is present in the balance and grace of the double helix, which most of us will only ever know as a drawing or a diagram. Some notion of harmony as well as of unpredictability is present in this creation story, this scientific tale of the generation of the heart of the world. In that respect this creation story shares elements with all other ones.

Creation stories are often specific to where they are told, so people can see every day the connecting patterns and designs that are in local creatures, vegetation, the sea and the sky. In some places indigenous Australians are divided up between saltwater and freshwater people. Perhaps we are all divided up in ways like this and linked to natural phenomena and forces. These may be the elements that we prefer in our daily lives, meat or fish, heat or cold, sun or shade, the sea or a river. Is it possible at this time of great global movements of people to find belonging and attachment in a vision of the whole world, in a fragment of tradition, in an intuition, in a series of correspondences, in a feeling that is not handed down but found? In order for people to not be divided into those who belong to certain places and those who do not, can we believe in the value of sharing food, respect for birds, animals, plants and trees, in responsibility for the planet?

If the most significant identity comes from land, what of those who have no land? Do they find it in embracing where they are, wherever that is? And what is the role of the first peoples? What can we learn from them?

Australian indigenous art draws on traditions and stories stretching back to what is often rather irritatingly called 'time immemorial'. It seems to stretch back to 'the beginning', to the moments when what is considered human came into being, was invented, discovered, found, imagined, created. This is the absolute first place of origin, the moment of the beginning of humanness, which coincides with the beginning of humans creating. This moment or series of moments is of intense interest to scientists who are always intensively looking for beginnings and explanations. The presence of what are the basic elements of art – charcoal, ochre, pigments, drawing and rituals – are the primary signs used by archaeologists to denote the quality of becoming human. Australia has been described as one of the first places where art and thus humanness began, in the sense of a discernible cognitive leap towards symbolic behaviour as evident in rock art drawings. Archaeologist Rhys Jones said: 'There was no long period of groping towards art. It was sudden. There was an extraordinary explosion of creativity.'

There is something miraculous in the survival of indigenous traditions and indigenous people all over the world. While they are still not always visible in the mainstream and it may have been possible even a few years ago to grow up without knowing of their survival, this is unlikely now. According to many indigenous accounts it is they who have in the past, and continue to in the present, ensured the survival of the earth or at least the parts of it in their care. The indigenous peoples who have survived into the twenty-first century contribute to cultural ecology, the diversity of possible cultural expressions that spells psychic health for humans as they keep alive different approaches to life and to the world. Just as the fertility of Bosch's Garden of Eden suggests an explosion of possible pathways to life, so diverse human cultures keep open the possibilities of what it is to be human.

The presence of indigenous people, indigenous culture and indigenous art means that we are surrounded by living extant knowledge of creation spirits and beings. We may need to seek it out, but once experienced it is rarely forgotten. It is like a blast of electricity to the soul. What does it mean, how does it matter? Rather than belonging to a distant or redundant past such beliefs and knowledge are present in contemporary life.

Indigenous people exist all over the world. The conviction expressed by them is radical. 'The trees are alive, the river is alive, the stones are alive,' are the words an indigenous man from Costa Rica said to me when I interviewed him in 1981 at the World Council of Indigenous Peoples conference in Canberra. I have never forgotten this, and the shiver that went through me when he said it. For I too believed it to be so, but had never said it aloud. Animism, totemism, identification with life forms beyond your own increase your empathy and respect for the world and embed you in a big family of relatives and relationships. The words we use to think about and describe such ideas are often found in anthropology, which took them from indigenous languages. Totem is a word from Ojibwa, an Algonquian language of the Great Lakes in North America. It translates as 'he is my relative'.

The impact of this kind of knowledge and conviction on Western attitudes of scepticism and empiricism is confronting in several ways. In asking for recognition of what is unable to be empirically seen or measured it asks for faith and trust. It also throws up the contingency of non-indigenous ways of seeing.

Thinking about a sentient earth has the effect of closing the gap between humans and the earth and her other inhabitants. Some version of animism is part of Western thought traditions (think of St Francis and many others) but has been set to one side for a long time.

When we enter the world, when we are born, we are aware of its animation. Spending time with a young child proves this fact. We arrive ready to find family and find it not only in humans. As we are acculturated we learn a particular way of seeing and thinking about the world, but where we come from, our origins, remain in this early identification with the world around us. This awareness belongs to all of us who live on the earth, and makes us indigenous. When dormant it may be re-awoken when we read about or hear indigenous peoples' descriptions of their beliefs. When an indigenous artist tells a story of how this piece of land was made it is his or her certainty and conviction as well as their artwork that impresses us with respect. We may or may not be able to fully believe what they tell us, but we believe that they believe.

There is an image that has remained with me for a long time. Actually it is not just in my mind but in a black and white photocopy on my shelf, and I like to look at it often as a touchstone of some kind. It is of a Native American garment called *Powhatan's Mantle*, once part of the seventeenth-century Tradescant Collection of Rarities (the first museum open to the public in England) now housed at the Ashmolean Museum in Oxford. It is supposed to have belonged to Powhatan, the father of Pocahontas, and is one of the earliest North American artefacts to have survived in a European museum. On this garment made from a buffalo, a tanned hide that retains the shape of an animal's body, a human figure is flanked by two animal forms and by many circles with concentric circles inside them like fingerprints. The design is stitched onto the hide in small white shell beads. To me the Mantle is a manifestation of a vision about the important and significant relationship between animal and human, and about common origins and common location on the earth, mutuality and sharing.

Even in silhouette we can recognise the forms of animals. It seems we have internalised their patterning and shapes. How do we visually distinguish animals from humans? Often by their ears, their 'creative' shapes, their imaginative forms – spots, stripes, horns, tails, manes, fur, ruffs. There is a rich variety in animal bodies that is not matched even by the many shades of colours or shapes that humans have. *Powhatan's Mantle* demonstrates in an object what I interpret as equivalence, symbiosis between animal and human. Totem: he is my relative. It is not necessarily possible to imitate the example set by indigenous people's totemic relationships with the world, but there is a level at which knowing about them and witnessing them leads us to thoughts of practical, prosaic and sometimes overwhelming obligation. If you think of a bird or an animal as your totem, your relative, how does it makes you feel?

Images that show when the world was made partake of a particular excitement; creation times are moments of great versatility when the way things are now was open to change. In the background of Bosch's painting there is a unicorn, a white (i.e. uncoloured) elephant and a white giraffe. It suggests that unicorns were there in the beginning, that elephants could have been orange and brown with spots and that giraffes could have been grey. Thus the arbitrariness and wonder of everything is emphasised as well as the aptness of the way things turned out. It is a puzzle that we know the answer to; it is an implicit benediction on all things.

At this time in the history of the world, we tend to see

ourselves as contributing to the destruction of the world rather than its creation. The scientific view of the creation of the world employs a mechanistic model in which either a big bang or a small whimper started it all, lightness/darkness, lightning and water, bacteria, photosynthesis, and in the water a stirring, a rim of green on a rock at the edge of the sea. Everything in the world is connected back to that moment and each time we see leaves or flowers breaking out from dead-seeming sticks, a tadpole stroking through the water, a bird dragging a piece of something to make a nest, we are there.

When it's hot the dog and I try to get our morning walk in early but don't always manage it. This means that on the way back from one of our half hour or hour long routes he will call a halt by stopping in the shade somewhere and flopping onto the ground and then rolling on his back in an effort to cool his skin. Dogs don't sweat through their skins, only through their mouths. I am hot too, of course, though wearing a hat, and would have gritted my teeth and pushed on rather than stopping but have learnt to respond to the moment, sit on the grass next to him and just enjoy being with a friend on a bit of dirt under a tree.

APRIL

finding water

*... when a glimmering of the mystery of time is given
in the darkness under a passing river.*
Toss Woolaston

Propped up somewhere in my studio is a book folded open to a page showing Caspar David Friedrich's painting *Monk by the Sea*. It has a coffee cup ring on its edge but the stain is no distraction from its solemnity. The painting's colours are a smoky grey blue, a greenish brown, white, and numerous greys from almost black to almost white. It shows mostly sky with cloud rolling over it, a narrow band of dark grey sea with some white-capped waves, a lighter band of chalky white sand and not much monk but it is the thoughts of the monk that I imagine when I look at it. He stands on the beach as if he is standing on the edge of the world. Dressed in a robe the colour of the sea, with his hand on his chin in a pose associated with thoughtfulness, perhaps because it suggests turning words that may have been spoken back into the mouth, he looks at the point where the sea meets the shore.

To some extent he reminds me of the cowled figure of Death in Ingmar Bergman's film *The Seventh Seal*. A film that my parents took me to see when I was very young and which absolutely terrified me, Death's pale looming face and the fear in the eyes of

April

the young witch burnt to death at the stake haunted my dreams for many nights and days. The visceral experience of pain and mystery pressed upon me by seeing both *The Seventh Seal* and *The Virgin Spring* at the same time (can they really have been on a double bill? I know it was at the Curzon in Goodwood Road where 'foreign' films were shown in the sixties in Adelaide) put scars on my psyche that have never faded. I remember being too shattered to sleep or go to school the next day, and instead walking on the beach in the morning discussing the films with my mother. What did the men do to the girl? Why would anyone burn another person while they are alive? What would the pain be like? Would death have to be so frightening? I don't remember her answers and barely remember the questions but I retain a sliver, less a snapshot than a split second, of memory that we walked on the beach and that the world seemed newly strange to me. It seems odd that I can't remember what she said, but I remember the sea on my left, the shore on my right and an edge of concrete wall next to a row of Norfolk pine trees.

The monk in Friedrich's painting is a Capuchin, an order of friars that began in 1525 as an offshoot of the Franciscan religious order formed by St Francis of Assisi around 1209. They pursue the simple life of contemplative prayer and poverty, chastity and obedience originally sought by St Francis. They are discalced, which means that they go barefoot, not even wearing sandals. I imagine that the monk has walked quite a way, kicking at the fabric of his long dark robe and feeling the sand slide beneath his feet. He stands there pondering, dwarfed by the sky which is in the process of silently shifting and tumbling with sea mist, cloud and light. For all its stillness the painting shows lots of movement, the slow rolling of the clouds, the steady back and forth and choppiness of the sea, the wheeling birds. It induces memories of breathing in the salty scent of sea air, as well as the noise and the commotion of walking in sand and then the silence of stopping to stand quietly in a place of constant movement. Some seagulls wheel around the monk, he contemplates air, a great silence, vast spaces, perhaps even, against his religion, a vision of death as annihilation or nothing, or as rejoining the continual flux around him rather than ascending to Heaven.

The mystery of the persistent silence of the sky is strongly present in the work. Apart from thunder and aeroplanes the sky is damn well silent, and yet it's so big. Each time you look at the sky if there are clouds and wind you see large movements carried out in complete and utter silence, a silence that somehow makes those movements even bigger and freer. This silent movement, whether slow, fast, twirling, circling or sliding, is both calming and expansive. You can lose your ability to judge distance while looking at the sky; and can travel great expanses with your eyes. Actually we all walk in the sky every day; the clouds share our space and we theirs. Sometimes they come and lie near us like pets and we call them fog, then they limit what we can see and they blanket sound.

In the beginning we came from the sea and our pulse answers to its continual movement. We are filled and reflected by the sea and the sky and we open up to embrace their largeness. Les Murray has written something about this opening with reference to the Australian hinterland: 'In the huge spaces of the outback, ordinary souls expand into splendid forms.' The word ordinary is significant here – it is not the exceptional, the extraordinary, the clever or the talented, that Murray is talking about, but the ordinary that expands into splendid forms or realises its inherent possession of them.

Yet the outback is not just huge space but also intimate space, plants and animals, and people, shadows and silences. Some need solitude, the sense of being unobserved by other humans, to feel free. In *The Road From Coorain* Jill Kerr Conway wrote about the country she grew up in, the western plains of New South Wales: 'Here, pressed into the earth by the weight of that enormous sky, there is real peace. To those who know it, the annihilation of the self, subsumed into the vast emptiness of nature, is akin to a religious experience.' And Randolph Stow wrote: 'Alone in the bush, with maybe a single crow ... a phrase like liberation of the spirit may begin to sound meaningful.' These descriptions suggest a state of simultaneous oblivion and location, a finding and a losing, a connection and a dissolving. Religious experience, liberation of the spirit, splendid forms – how are these things connected to wide open spaces? Is there an inevitable human response to such spaces? If the space is not thought of as empty, does that make it more or less spiritual or religious? Is such a space one in which you expand both metaphorically and actually as you feel your equivalence or kinship with cloud, rock and tree?

In *Monk by the Sea* there is an intense mixture of sadness and ecstasy in this confrontation of a religious person, a human who has declared their commitment to God, with the immense power of the sea and the sky. In 1810 when the painting was first shown poet Heinrich von Kleist famously described it as making him feel as if he had no eyelids. Later art historian Wieland Schmidt described it as an image of infinity, a painting that does not finish with its frame: 'The shore, the sea and the sky extend endlessly on either side ...'

Another painting by Friedrich that is very intense in its evocation of a full emptiness is *The Large Enclosure at Dresden*, which also shows a great deal of sky though at least twice as much land as *Monk by the Sea*. The Large Enclosure was a swamp to the north-west of Dresden near the Elbe and the Weisseritz rivers. It was a hunting ground with three great alleys of linden trees planted in 1744 running through it. Today it is planted with factories and a large harbour. In Friedrich's time in the 1800s the trees were still there, but it was also a piece of boggy land left open to the sky. In German the painting is called *Das Grosse Gehege*. The word *Gehege* means an animal enclosure; thus it has the sense of describing a piece of land preserved like a national park. Being so close to a swamp the land was liable to flood. And in the huge European floods of 2002 the Weisseritz river did leave its canalised bed near the inner city and flow in its old run right through Dresden directly towards the Elbe river.

There is great spaciousness in *The Large Enclosure*, but for all this ecstatic openness it is very sombrely coloured apart from a band of yellow in the sky. It is that particular elusive shade of yellow with an egg-yolky orange tinge that sometimes hangs about for a while after the sun has set. Below the yellow is a dense bank of purple cloud and a series of smaller purple clouds which echo the shapes beneath them on the land of patches of water dispersed over dark olive grey mud. The colourlessnesses of darkness, the multiple greys that fill the night, have begun to fall on the earth but are not yet apparent in the sky. The water reflects the pale blue almost grey of the sky with a luminous white glow that is slightly more intense towards the centre of the painting. In the sky the new moon can just be seen in an edge of mauve cloud. The water on the earth curves towards the place where the sun has slipped beneath the horizon, while the long bank of purple clouds in the sky curve up from that place. Thus a series of rhythms, resonances, correspondences and reflections is set up and the viewer is embraced by the very curve of the earth made visible.

The reflection of the sky in the water on the ground means that light both lies on and is reflected up from the ground, but there are patches of dark land in this skywater so that there

April

is a perforation, a mixing up of solidity and fluidity, a balance between soft and hard. I think of this painting as an image of a heart – its interlocking of land, water and sky reminds me of diagrams of ventricles and aortas, veins and arteries, the blue and the red systems running next to each other, taking in oxygen, expelling carbon dioxide, precise, but full of the intense organic unpredictable irregularity of emotion. Near the middle of the painting a boat with its sail hanging down is becalmed in the water, a single tree behind it is like its companion. The boat cannot keep going but will have to turn back or stay and wait for the river to flow. It is a human presence in this quiet scene in which the slow beauty of the long moment of twilight is present, and in which the inevitable measured emerging of the stars is just about to occur. The low level of water means that the bed of the river, something usually not seen, is visible. Perhaps the boat has come this far just to see that light, and that darkness.

Some of the mood of *The Large Enclosure* is echoed in *Flood on the Darling 1890*, by far the best painting ever made by W.C. Piguenit. The huge floods in 1890 in the west of New South Wales meant that the Darling River, normally a measly ten to twenty metres wide, spread to as much as sixty-five kilometres across. The painting does not deal at all with the human disaster of the flood but with the transformation of the land into a place of watery beauty and wonder. It shows distant trees reflected in water with a foreground of marooned grassy green islands. The late afternoon sky is overall whitish grey, with a sun hidden behind layers of grey clouds that it illuminates in a hazy intense way. On the water the light creates a silvery skin that almost merges with the sky in the distance. The reflections of the clouds stretch in white glowing blurs across the water. In the foreground waterbirds can be seen fishing and standing in the weedy shallows. On the horizon is a very significant part of the painting, a line of pure white silvery light. So your eyes are held between grey-white clouds suffused with light and reflected silvery-grey light on water, and that long line of whiteness in the far distance where the sun hits the water in a moment of pure dissolving, of being unable to see anything at all. As if looking at a mirage, your eyes are suspended in light.

These two paintings, made more than sixty years apart, one in Europe and one in Australia, induce the same physiological sensations, a deep breathing of the eyes, a movement and a release, travelling deep into painted space to connect with big impersonal forces and to feel them intimately. Friedrich's *The Large Enclosure* was made in a swampy country prone to floods where water seeps up. Piguenit's *Flood on the Darling* was painted in a dry country marked by dry riverbeds and very occasional floodings that mark the land with water patterns. Each of them connects water and sky, human and earth, in an ancient relationship of attachment.

We go early and enter the park by climbing under and through the two-rail wooden fence. Dogs are not allowed here but we come anyway. Some people say dogs should be allowed in national parks because the Aborigines had dingoes for the last 2000 to 3000 years. Today rainbow lorikeets are flashing green and pink at us everywhere as they fly sideways out of the dusty dry creekbed and through the grey-green trees. We stop to examine a dead, bearded dragon lizard body; its colour is the same as the white-grey earth, its scales so tiny they are like toast crumbs. I would never have seen its flat thin dry body without the dog to show me. Under a bush we see dog faeces which have become like pure white chalk in the sun.

MAY

the place of the dead

There are many stars, more than we can count. We need the stars, they give us light. And people — we all need each other. There are many sorts of people: we need them all.
Gulumbu Yunupingu

Here and there propped up around our house among other things are images of Aboriginal art, mnemonics, memory notes, for what they make me think about and what I love in them; a postcard of *Untitled* 1989 by Emily Kame Kngwarreye from the Queensland Art Gallery, an image of a bark painting by Nanganaralil of the Djambarrpuyngu clan collected by Dr Helen Groger-Wurm from Milingimbi in 1967, and an out-of-date *Art Almanac* folded open on a page showing a bark by Wandjuk Marika in an advertisement for Sotheby's.

Emily's work is of a type she did that I recall first seeing with a sense of aha! At the time that she began painting in 1988 there was a lot of talk about secret sacred meanings in Aboriginal paintings and the particular style of her work evident in the postcard seems to embrace the idea of demonstrating secrecy because patterns of dots and lines can clearly be seen to be covering other layers of dots and lines beneath them. What is hidden is not clear but it is clear that it is hidden. It's a very clever work with multiple textures and densities of paint and colour. It is a kind of beautiful hiding in the light full of a mixture of transparency and opacity, movement and stillness. There's a network of semi-transparent white lines like a series of walking tracks, and then there are semi-circular places where the white lines converge. There are green dots and grey dots and dark red and pale pink ones; the dots cover everything but the tracery of lines beneath them is visible. Also it is an early work made before Emily was slamming paintings out at a great rate, though a feature of her way of painting was always to work quickly and even impatiently. She began by painting batik, a medium much too laboured and time-consuming for someone with her temperament. In her retrospective where her work was arranged chronologically it was possible to discern the actual moment when she broke away from trying to be careful and neat and simply painted the way she felt like doing it.

Cut from an Australian Information Service calendar of 1982, the complex untitled bark painted by Nanganaralil in red and brown ochre, and in black and white, tells a complex story of life and death involving a crow, a praying mantis, a lizard, a hollow log coffin and a cabbage palm tree, but one of the main reasons it appeals to me is because it includes a figure (the crow) with arms and legs like a human but the head of a bird so that it looks like a cartoon character or like an Egyptian god, thus embracing metamorphosis and species interchangeability, that hybridity shared by legends and cartoons. And it reminds me of the first screenprint that I ever made at Megalo International Silkscreen Collective Workshop in 1981. It was called *Hard luck and troubles coming on after me* (named from a blues song for the path that it was clear I was going to follow, as I decided to enter art school rather than the Public Service for which I was accepted at the same time). It included a bird-headed figure and a bear-headed one, the bird dancing and the bear seated in an armchair toasting with a golden cup, both wrapped in the joy of the moment and the certain knowledge of difficulty ahead.

Wandjuk Marika's bark called *Djan'Kawu at Yalan'bara* (1959) shows rows and rows of people and rows and rows of fish. Of course it is a creation story. It is painted in black and red and white, but there is an especially large amount of yellow in it and I like to look at it because to me it is as if the yellow might take over and the whole thing will dissolve in yellow ochre's soft luminescence. I could learn more about it but don't wish to right now. I just like to look at the vibrating energy of the yellow.

I remember the excitement of visiting the 'Primitive Art' basement gallery of the Art Gallery of New South Wales in the late seventies and early eighties and responding to the very strong sense of presences and spirits within the objects of Aboriginal and Pacific art displayed in that dim underground cave. It was a place which made you hold your breath and feel a bit scared that you might be possessed by some of the intense energy emanating from the works. This was clearly where the power and life in the gallery lay, and it was put below ground and in the dark in order to mute it and keep it under control. That basement gallery is no longer entered or used in that way, though the research library which now occupies the basement maintains the strange tradition of keeping Pacific culture underground. Marvellous shields, whose makers are unrecorded, hang in the foyer at the bottom of the white marble stairs that you descend to reach the library.

In 1994 Yiribana opened as the official Indigenous Cultures Gallery at the Art Gallery of New South Wales. Among the most famous and precious works that were displayed in a courtyard off Yiribana are the *Tutini*, seventeen *pukamani* or grave posts from Melville Island made in the late fifties by Laurie Nelson Tukialila,

AN OPENING

Bob One Galadingwama, Big Jack Yarunga, Don Durak Madjua, Charlie Quiet Kwangdini and an unknown artist. Commissioned and donated to the Gallery by Stuart Scougall in 1958, they were originally placed on show in the Art Gallery foyer by curator and artist Tony Tuckson before they were moved down to the 'Primitive Art' basement where I first saw them. The last time I saw them in 2010 they were right amongst the historic art collection, though not juxtaposed with contemporaneous works but with works showing the first encounters of Aboriginal and European cultures and the first European paintings of Australia made in the 1800s.

If fulfilling their normal task of commemoration of a death on Melville Island the *Tutini* would have weathered and by now be a silvery-grey colour and rotting on the ground, but as they have been protected from the weather they are still vividly coloured. Their white, yellow, red and black painted patterns of circles, half-circles, dots and lines are fresh and lively, they communicate grace, integrity, immediacy, energy, qualities all found in the natural world and here turned into cultural objects that respond to it on those terms. Whenever I saw them there was no adjacent wall panel translating or explaining them in detail, yet as they are grave posts it is clear that there is some recording or accounting of life and death, and the transition between them, present in their marks; in other words the kind of reflections and feelings which attend funerals. Without any explanatory notes provided what is clear is that the paintings and carvings on the *Tutini* are human sign systems organising and speaking with great energy and graphic power. In the glowing primary natural earth colours of yellow and red, black and white, the designs are animated and rhythmical and speak of the structures of human thought as pattern-making. Here are multiple rows of white dots on a black ground banded with strong red stripes; here yellow dots

May

alternate with the white reminding me of pollen, of rain, of stars; here red diamond shapes are linked by bars of white edged with black; here red lines criss-cross white, here black; here red circles are filled with yellow dots and surrounded by haloes of white. Here a wash of colour retains the marks of its application, thus making us think of its making by hand over time. Though the works are carefully made they are not at all laboured or painstaking but possess great freshness and lightness of touch. Though they are grave posts they are made with a sense of joy. They possess a lot of what curator Judith Ryan wrote recently about finding in bark painting: 'The greatest bark painting contains a sensibility of design and surface texture, an inner life, a vital rhythm in the drawing ... its power is not the result of technical facility or neatness, but the reverse.'

The Aboriginal Memorial, two hundred hollow log coffins made by artists from Ramingining and surrounding areas in Central Arnhem Land, one for each year of European settlement in Australia, was first shown at the *7th Biennale of Sydney* in 1988 at Pier 2/3, Walsh Bay, a place full of the scent and sight of the sea entering through gaps in the wooden walls and floor of the old wharf building, and flowing to and fro, catching and glimmering in the light. After this first historic showing *The Aboriginal Memorial* was bought by the National Gallery in Canberra. The log coffins, a powerful artwork commemorating death, echo the *Tutini*. Each brings part of a mortuary ceremony into a prominent position in a major art gallery, each affirms culture and connection to place, each is made from trees and is a vertical memorial linking sky and land. *The Aboriginal Memorial* is the first work on show in the National Gallery of Australia in Canberra, so the vitality of its earth colours and the teeming life-forms depicted on them are the first things you see when you enter.

The Aboriginal Memorial commemorates all the indigenous

people who, since 1788, have lost their lives defending their land — thus it is arguably a war memorial. The log coffins commemorate continuity with the past as well as ongoing cultural strength. Forty-three artists from nine different clans of Yolngu people, each the caretakers of a specific site around the Glyde River, painted them. Such ceremonial hollow-log coffins are still used in mortuary ceremonies to hold the bones of the deceased, but these ones were made only for display as artworks. Like so many Aboriginal artworks they are virtual title deeds to the land. The path that can be walked through the coffins is the course of the Glyde River in the Northern Territory; the coffins are set out according to where the clans live along the river; its tributaries and geographical features, the flora and fauna of each of those places are shown on the coffins. There are the swamp or Magpie Goose people, the mangrove people, the people of the eucalyptus forest who are also the sugarbag (honey) people, the stone country people, the Morning Star people, the freshwater people and others. Stories connecting places and people are implicit: thus a series of striped coffins refer to the mud lines on trees caused by water moving in and out on the edge of the tidal flats. There are images here that we can recognise and others that we need some teaching to understand. A catfish may be easy to recognise with its whiskery head, though knowing it is a symbol of both new life and death is an added dimension. Recognising diamond patterns as honeycomb, wavy or straight line patterns as tides and water or/and clouds and rain or/and fire and smoke may need some coaching, though a bit of instruction makes the viewing very satisfying and makes it possible to begin to see the complexity in its simplicity.

Within coo-ee of the dancing lights and salt air of Sydney Harbour, *Edge of the Trees*, a collaborative artwork designed by artists Fiona Foley and Janet Laurence in 1995 and located outside the Museum of Sydney, echoes both these significant artworks, *Tutini* at the Art Gallery of New South Wales and *The Aboriginal Memorial* at the National Gallery of Australia. *Edge of the Trees* was commissioned by curator Peter Emmett to respond to the site of the first Government House in Australia, to represent first contact between two cultures and to draw attention to the connected histories of black and white people in Australia since 1788. Emmett used a quote from archaeologist Rhys Jones to inspire and direct the artists:

> ... *the discoverers struggling through the surf were met on the beach by other people looking at them from the edges of the trees. Thus the same landscape perceived by the newcomers as alien, hostile or having no coherent form was to the indigenous people their home, a familiar place, the inspirer of dreams.*

Eloquent and spare, these twenty-seven posts, made from sandstone, steel or wood, some rusted, some charred with fire, contain sound elements so that the soft voices of Aboriginal people murmur words and names to you as you walk through or stand near them. They evoke the ordinary everyday artefacts of wooden telegraph poles, symbols of communication and the crossing of distance, as well as train lines and bridge girders, gravestones and steles. Seashells mixed with ash, honey mixed with wax, feathers, oxides, fishbones and crab claws entwined in hair, pipeclay, seeds and resin are captured in glass chambers in the sides of some of the poles. And words, words are everywhere, engraved into wood and stone, and etched into metal, reiterating what is lost and what is remembered. There are names of Aboriginal people and of the members of the First Fleet, there are names of plants in Latin, in English and in Aboriginal languages. The work draws attention to a sense of encounters and interactions across borders. It focuses on the firsthand experience of materials and artefacts that we know by touch, but above all it is language, written down but most vividly present as sound in the murmuring voices, which enters your ears and vibrates in your body, powerfully evoking the intangible nature of memory and emotion.

Each of these three major artworks are important icons of Australian art; they speak of death and life; and they pin down important historical moments with precision as well as being guides, teaching aids, about respect, knowledge and the distinct presence of past and present Aboriginal countries in Australia.

Many people see Aboriginal art as for other Aboriginal people, or anthropologists, or tourists looking for something authentically Australian. Yet its recurring themes of close knowledge of land and place, as well as stories of diaspora and dispossession, actually have distinct affiliations with the experience of people all over the world, especially many who have ended up in Australia. The importance of identity, of language and of belonging, is highly significant to today's mass movements of people. And an ecological approach to life necessitates seeing the planet in a custodial way, with a strong awareness of symbiosis with it, something which indigenous cultures all over the world have always practised. In 2008 in Melbourne Paraguayan art critic Ticio Escobar told me that the Guarani, an indigenous people of the South American interior, say that the bush is their supermarket, their pharmacy and their church. They consider only country that has never been cleared or farmed to be truly alive.

Today the dog and I walk along Alexandra Avenue in the late afternoon past the many nineteenth-century houses in the suburb of Rose Park and shuffle through the oak leaves scattered on the ground in great yellow and silver piles. At the end of one of the long avenues of trees I see a stone holding a metal plaque saying Fallen Soldiers Memorial Trees and a list of names. Then I notice each elm tree has a disc driven into the ground next to it with a small cross and a name upon it. All along the wide grassed corridor that lies between the oak tree-lined street seventy-five English elms were planted in 1919, each for a man from here who died in the First World War. How many times have I driven past, seeing and liking the avenue as especially shady, long and evoking Europe, but not aware of the trees' commemorative function? The dog burrows into the leaves, they release a soft scent — and I remember how once long ago I filled my pockets with dry oak leaves while walking home from school and put them in a cardboard box in my room in an attempt to retain their bittersweet elusive fragrance.

JUNE
a leaf from my book

A thing seen is more believable and long-lasting to us than something we hear.
Albrecht Dürer

Hanging over the mantelpiece in my bedroom is a framed reproduction of a drawing made by Albrecht Dürer in 1512. I bought it in 1972 at the Albertina Museum in Vienna. On the same trip I went to Nuremberg where Dürer lived for the last nineteen years of his life and placed my hands on the outside wall of his house and silently implored some kind of sympathetic magic to connect me with his spirit. As I had failed to get into art school in 1970 my continuing belief in my destiny to be an artist was for me a kind of shameful secret involving extremes of failure and success. The dream was more feeling and desire than either accomplishment or hard work. My desire was to create, to bring into being, to make exterior and visible what was interior and invisible, to catch a flame of wonder and set down a moment of understanding, to communicate. I was also inspired by the idea of not knuckling down into some conventional existence but to live to the full in making artwork and never to stop, to never retire but always be creating, to never compromise and always to be understood by others through the work. If words and social

June

skills failed me the work would stand in for any incompetence, and thus friendships and relationships would be based on true knowledge rather than a façade.

This decision was made early in life. I remember confirming it to myself while sitting in the back seat of the family car, in the usual tense silence, somewhere between Sydney and Adelaide, looking out to see the curve of a half-ploughed field divided by a sweeping line, intense green on one side, red-brown on the other. I took a deep breath and thought I definitely know what I want to do, that's what I will do with my life, show and convey this intensity, this feeling in my heart and gut that this abrupt edge of colour gives me, this visible place of transformation. This was a good feeling, not an act but a decision, but to really belong to me it was important that it remain secret. A secret was a talisman, a source of strength, a place of safety.

Yet how much of a secret was it? My perception of it is that no-one knew, yet … as a young child I continually asked my grandparents for paints for Christmas and was continually disappointed in getting those hard dry pans of watercolour paints to which water has to be applied and then the paint carefully worked up to get a small amount of watery paint. These paints suggested the making of decorous, careful, slow 'good' paintings with fine brushes, not big, energetic, fast 'bad' paintings. A bit like the situation at primary school in Austria where we children (or was it just the girls?) were told that we were meant to be like violets, humble and sweet-smelling with drooping heads, not like roses, proud, stiff and beautiful (but I want to be a rose, I cried).

I persisted with the paint idea and asked my grandparents for paint in tubes and got small silvery metal tubes of watercolour paint. They were tubes but it was still hard to be extravagant with them. I longed to have big fat tubes and squeeze out great thick lumps of paint and really move it around. I did not want to learn how to paint, to follow rules or to become good at following rules. Art was not about rules. Art was about freedom and feelings. If you wanted rules you should be a policeman or a judge.

I had known thick paint, for in 1961, when I was seven, the whole family went on a skiing holiday in Austria and I was asked by a group of young people staying at the same hotel what I wanted to be when I grew up. My main companion at the time was a large teddy bear, with articulated limbs and a growl box, who was almost as big as I was. He was a replacement for an earlier lamb which had been lost by being accidentally flushed down the toilet. My agitation at this loss had my parents driving me around the streets of San Francisco looking for the lamb I had been attached to since birth which of course they knew wasn't out walking the streets or having a meal in a diner but stuck in a pipe or heading out to some sewage treatment plant. In despair they introduced me to Teddy, a toy belonging to my older sister that she was not interested in, and that was that. We were inseparable, sleeping and travelling together. His wise glass eyes, his black nose, yellowish fur, his velvet paws and straw stuffing gave him many qualities, both sensual and philosophic.

Years later in Austria the young people in the hotel we were staying in took an interest in me and asked me what I wanted to be or do most of all. An artist I replied. So much for my secret, yet this was before that decisive moment in front of an Australian field of green growth and red earth. Maybe we were snowed in or there was not enough good snow, but somehow they got some really fat tubes of oil paint and some paper and set me up at a table overlooking the mountains. What shall I paint was my question, what do you love was the answer. Thus I painted a life-size portrait of my beloved friend Teddy in thick yellow ribbons of paint.

When we left the hotel this painting of a strong body and head covered in yellow fur with a red and blue background was placed in the back window of the car for our further travelling. As it didn't dry quickly and smelled a lot and smudged everything around it with oily paint, after much swearing it was carefully folded and thrown in a bin. When you are travelling through the mountains having a large wet oil painting on paper in your Hillman Minx is not so great, so sadly the painting was thrown away before it got back to Vienna. I recall no pain at losing the work though I must have been upset; I do remember how he grew to fill the page and then onto another sheet and how thick the paint was and how rich its texture and colour.

The print of Dürer's drawing that hangs over my mantelpiece is called *Wing of a Blue Roller*. It shows the wing of a bird, *Coracias garrulous*, also known as a European Roller, a bird noted for its blue plumage of shades ranging from pale turquoise to dark ultramarine, with bright reddish-brown on its back. It is called a roller owing to its habit of 'rolling', turning over in flight like a tumbler pigeon. Rollers live in Europe but go to Africa for the European winter.

Dürer has written the date 1512 above the wing and below it the D inside an A that is his signature, both in reddish ink. He would have used a finely pointed feather, probably a goose quill, to write it. The drawing shows the wing realistically but not hyper-real, it is visibly as much a drawing as a painting. The wing is painted on vellum, an early alternative to paper, the processed hide of an animal characterised by its thin smooth durable properties and giving a certain luminosity to a drawing. The large areas of colour are laid down softly with a broad brush and transparent watercolour paint, then delicate lines are drawn over them with a very finely sharpened quill dipped in opaque gouache paint. The drawing shows the layering of feathers that make up a wing, the progression from the stiffer longer flight feathers with their firm shapes to the soft shorter feathers on the body of the bird. The colour of the feathers changes, sometimes gently and sometimes abruptly, from dark blue almost black tips to a lighter blue and then to a very pale blue that is almost white. The painting shows the small overlapping feathers on the shoulder of the wing which outline and pad the bones and are akin to the scales on fish or snakes, evidence of the connection between the bird and other species. The rainbow iridescence of the feathers is suggested by a tremulous quality in the colours like shot silk; the turquoise glints with red, the red glints with blue. The entire drawing is alive with the harmony and rhythm of the wing and its colouring, the evidence of Dürer's close observational skills, in the care he has taken in recording it and in a release from total precision at the same time, an absorption in detail has allowed him some ecstasy at its depiction. The work is precise but it is not a cold precision, rather a joyful graphic facility that emanates delight and affection.

Whilst celebrated for his extraordinary imaginative and detailed woodcuts and copperplate engravings of mythological and religious subjects like his three Master engravings *The Knight, Death, and the Devil* (1513), *Melencolia I*, and *St Jerome in his Study* (both 1514), in this drawing of a bird's wing Dürer has created a work that is somehow private; it is both miraculous and intimate, personal and communicative. It quietly holds beauty, tranquillity and wonder. This beauty is available to everyone in contemplating something as simple, as complex, as ordinary or extraordinary as a dead bird's wing, or indeed an insect or a flower. The gesture of the wing is one of expansion and ascension – it is like an open hand. I have always seen this wing drawing as breathtakingly beautiful and tender, and a symbol of aspiration – something that Icarus may have had on his wall.

In 1961–2 my family lived in Austria. We stayed in an old

June

Hapsburg castle called Schloss Hernstein, forty-five minutes from Vienna, for the end of the winter, the spring and the beginning of the summer. We were to live in a new apartment in Vienna, but as it was still being built the bank that was building the apartment offered us accommodation in the castle that they owned. The yellow-painted Schloss was surrounded by massive green-painted wrought-iron fences with a formal stone entrance, a sweeping circular drive, a great wooden door through which a coach could be driven into the castle's courtyard, many green-painted wrought-iron lightposts with cast metal statues of green lions holding them up, a lake with an island and large grounds with walking trails to sculptures and an artificial ruin above the castle. Here my sister and I worked with a governess learning to speak and write German in preparation for attending local schools in Vienna. We also learnt embroidery, knitting and crochet, and spent a lot of time outside. An old man and his wife were the caretakers of the castle, and while she showed us how to make apricot dumplings and gave us crushed garlic on bread and dripping to eat, he carved wooden spoons for us, three of which I still have, and wove wastepaper baskets from wood shavings, one of which I still use. The base of the bin is a piece of thick cardboard cut from an old advertising poster. I remember how he cut it from the dark blue and white spotted skirt of a woman, and how it was and is still possible to see the swinging movement of her skirt in the fragment he cut from it. The rhythms of castle life included stopping at the nearby village to buy special strawberry lollies, growing vegetables and keeping rabbits, catching butterflies and tadpoles, picking flowers, walking or skiing through the grounds and watching the green sludge of the lake being dredged from a raft.

My mother encouraged us to keep diaries to make some record of our experiences. We generally ignored this idea, though we both kept autograph books. In Austria this was a serious business, as thoughts of mortality pervaded society and primary school children were very stern and would think nothing of drawing a wreath and writing a verse about death in your autograph book. Under the Gothic St Stefan's Cathedral in the heart of Vienna human skeletons were on view in the cold dank sulphurous catacombs, and great quantities of yellowy-white wax with which we made spooky, long fingernails could be collected from under the many votive candles. Another child, our friend and apartment neighbour Nora, showed us all these treats. She had decided to be a vegetarian early in life and was very pale and thin with what looked like dark pink bruises under her eyes and especially long dark brown hair. When we played Cowboys and Indians she was Pocahontas with her long thin plait. One day in the apartment playing a game we all pushed against a glass door and she went through the glass and inside her arm the flesh was pink and sponge-like.

In my autograph book a girl at school drew a neat spray of heart-shaped flowers with coloured pencils and wrote *Lern denken mit den Herz und fühlen mit den Geist* (learn to think with your heart and to feel with your spirit) quoting German novelist and poet Theodor Fontane. Another girl quoted Goethe: *Willst du immer weiter schweifen? Sieh, das Gute liegt so nah, lerne nur das Glück ergreifen, denn das Glück ist immer da.* (Why are you always travelling further? See, what is good is so near, only learn to hold onto luck and luck will always be there.)

I felt she was unfairly accusing me of being shiftless when I was after all only a young child and had to go with my family wherever they went, whether they were shiftless or not. That girl was especially neat in her hair, dress and manner and had developed a stencil technique of drawing where you cut out a shape then fill in small blocks of coloured pencil around the edge of it. Then you place it coloured side up where you want it and rub the colour onto the page either with your finger or another piece of paper. Thus the crisp outline of the shape is surrounded by tiny soft clouds of multiple colours.

Unlike the neat hearts and flowers of my school companions, the few drawings that I did of the insects, flowers and mushrooms that I saw around me in the castle garden were rough and crude. I often broke pencils by pressing too hard and was really better with oil crayons. My drawings show water bugs, bees, beetles, and different flowers and mushrooms, each with a number to accompany them and a key listing their names. These were partly in imitation of the primers we used to learn German and our guidebooks for birds and mushrooms. These drawings in a small yellow and black padded book are one of the few things left from that time, apart from the wooden spoons and the wastepaper basket and some photographs which show how the upstairs staterooms of the castle which we very rarely went into had dark polished wooden floors and were flushed with red-gold light. In the photos we stand pale, stiff and small against their glowing golden beauty. In the warmer weather we ate outside under a big spreading linden tree and when we were outside everything was always better, the food tasted good and anxiety was dissipated. That spring and summer was a wonderful season of flowers and watching growth from the earth, being close to and studying water and trees, dragonflies and tadpoles. Perhaps for each child there is one special spring and that was mine. A soft green European one.

At high school in Australia in 1968 I was graded as far too intelligent to study art and placed in a Latin class. After spectacular failure at Latin I received special dispensation to leave the Latin scholars four times a week and study art with the other non-Latin students, who were generally considered beyond redemption. Art was seen as vaguely therapeutic but not useful in any way. The art room was a place with few rules and little instruction – certainly no art history was taught – but what I recall is an almost empty room with a row of tall windows letting in lots of light, desks, and a row of fat cardboard tube containers full of powdered paint in acid green, red, black, yellow and blue, which we mixed with PVA glue to make different colours. I liked using oil crayons and then covering the drawing with paint which would roll off the crayon in a patchy way. Once, using this technique, I drew a picture of people decorated with feathers and body paint dancing around a fire, a war-dance or corroboree; it was rewarded with an A and mounted by the teacher on a piece of red cardboard. Another one of my prize-winning works was King Arthur's magic sword Excalibur being caught over the lake, a complex swirl of green and blue with a cut-out arm clutching the sword pasted on top.

One day we did linocuts and I had a sharp introduction to printmaking when I pressed a curved blade deep into my thumb when thoughtlessly pushing it onto the tool-holder. After being bandaged I cut out a radiant sun. I recall experiencing two epiphanies in the art room; one was when drawing a cow's skull in charcoal that while I worked gradually took on the form and more than that, the spirit of the skull. This also happened with a rose. As I drew the lines I followed what I saw with my charcoal to show the rose's petals folded and unfolded around its heart and somehow it came to life. This looking and transcribing was a transformational event as the drawing somehow broke away from its source to own its own volume and meaning. To me this is like Dürer's experience with the Blue Roller wing. His drawing possesses affection as well as wonder, joy as well as skill. He was equally engaged with his ability and the magical way life could be re-created with it, as with the infinite diversity and beauty of nature.

June

Dürer is the only artist known to have recorded his admiration for the Aztec treasures sent by Cortés from Mexico in 1520, which he saw when they were on show in Brussels. He wrote in his diary commenting on 'the wonderful works of art and subtle displays of ingenuity of people in faraway lands' that 'were much more beautiful to me than miracles'. In his view it was not necessary for an artwork to be laboured over to possess life:

A man may often draw something with his pen on a half-sheet of paper in one day or engrave it with his tool on a small block of wood, and it shall be fuller of art and better than another's great work on which he has spent a whole year's careful labour.

Dürer's wing says to me that art is not labour but love.

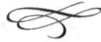

The dog and I like to walk at dawn, in the early evening and at night. At dawn the earth is exhaling and there is more scent for him to smell, left over from the night travels of animals, and for me a fresh dampness in the air that carries more scent than the day's drier air. In the early evening we smell dinners cooking and see into lighted rooms looking to see what pictures people have hanging on their walls, but at night we could be anywhere, the sky is a deep purple rather than black or grey – maybe it never really is grey or black except in artworks. We walk under wheeling stars through darkness and find a place to be.

JULY

measuring the world

As a woman, I have no country ...
As a woman my country is the world.
Virginia Woolf

Several pages cut from calendars have watched over the childhood of my son Jerome.

I carried them with me from Canberra to Adelaide, from the site of his conception to the site of his birth. That year when we moved together into my old bedroom in my mother's house I taped them to the wall where they stayed for the next fifteen or so years. We looked at them many times and they became part of the furniture of our lives. If I see one of them illustrated in a book it is as if a part of me is there.

I cut them from two calendars published in 1982 and 1986 by the Australian Information Service. My favourite, now on my office wall, is a powerful bark painting by an artist called simply Nanjewara. It was collected on Groote Eylandt by the Czech artist and collector Karel Kupka in 1963 and is in the collection of the National Gallery of Australia. It is a marvellous image in red, black and white of stars in the sky. Painted on a black background is a red ochre circle along the edge of which are seven red frogs reaching out. Around them in the night sky are twelve

July

large red ochre stars with white points and inside the circle like constellations are two eels or snakes and two fish as well as a circular stem from which stems of yellow and white star-like flowers sprout. It is an explosive, energetic image that speaks of creation and metamorphosis, of the exultation and consolation of viewing the night sky loaded with stars. And of learning the stars to navigate or tell stories and drawing imaginary lines between them to make images in order to find a way through what seems so illimitable and complex. I was so attached to it that I kept the calendar as well as the image. The story it tells is that the painting represents a legend from Groote Eylandt and shows a waterhole surrounded by frogs which later went into the sky and became stars like the Southern Cross. The stars within the circle are stars reflected in the water.

In 1973 I visited Groote Eylandt. My father was working there in the Gulf of Carpentaria doing a consultancy for a mining company that involved studying the tides and currents. He had imported his oceanographic measuring meters from Russia. Getting through the airport with timers ticking inside weighty metal cylinders about the size of a small fire extinguisher covered in Russian writing was part of the fun. I was at the University of Adelaide studying classical studies, philosophy, politics, history and English when he rang and said to ask his secretary to book a ticket for me to visit in my holidays. On the light plane from Darwin to Groote there were both Aboriginal and non-Aboriginal people, and I still recall how uncomfortable I felt when the non-Aboriginal men spoke disparagingly and unpleasantly to me about the Aboriginal people who seemed to look ashamed for them.

On Groote my father was staying in a white, wooden house on stilts with louvres and mosquito mesh on all sides and lots of ceiling fans. The temperature was the same inside and outside your body so that having a shower made you feel invisible or as if you might be about to wash away. We went to a BBQ and I found that drinking lots of beer, holding the can in a special foam sleeve, a stubbie holder, so that it did not get hot from being held in your hand, was very easy. I had a wakeful night and told my father the next day; he was amused and said that that can happen with alcohol. No matter, for I had plenty of time to doze during the day when we went out in the *Arabia*, the slow diesel boat of Gerry Blitner, to check tide and current meters tucked under rocks or hanging from buoys out in the Gulf. The boat moved at about two kilometres an hour so that we would see where we were headed and then know it would take a few hours to get there. We put long fishing lines with shiny lures on them to trawl off the back of the boat for large silver fish which we pulled in and ate immediately, either quickly fried or raw and whitened with lemon juice. At various times I was put ashore on a rock outcrop with an Aboriginal man to do some rock-fishing. One thing that my father asked me to bring with me was some saffron in order to make bouillabaisse, and one night we made it with at least four or five different kinds of fish as well as shellfish, including the amazing thick-shelled Moreton Bay bugs.

From the boat we saw an island with a rock formation on it that looked like a turtle (I was asked what I thought it was called – everyone expected me to get the answer), this was the home island of my fishing companion. He was sad that he could not live there any more – no-one did – and we went onto it with him to view rock paintings of birds, kangaroos and handprints hidden between vertical rocks. Recently I found out that it was Chasm Island, where in 1803 William Westall who travelled with Matthew Flinders on the *Investigator* made watercolour drawings of Aboriginal rock art, said to be the first Aboriginal art seen by Europeans.

July

I recall bits and pieces of my visit, like when we had to cross a waist-deep, narrow creek and the Aboriginal men told me it had crocodiles in it and all laughed and laughed when I crossed it especially quickly; and when we stopped the car so someone could chase a frill-necked lizard and put it on the road so that I could photograph it and then they put it back on a tree upside down so that its tail hung over its head and we all laughed at the expression on its face; and when we drove my fishing friend home to the Umbakumba Mission where he lived and my father stopped to give some women a lift the man had to get off and walk because he was not allowed to be with them (one of them was his mother-in-law or something like that); and I recall my father's disgust at the Aboriginal peoples' living conditions compared to those of the white people, and the small whites-only club. I remember seeing vivid green tree ants swarming over vines, and I recall walking in the shallow water of the sea and being closely followed by a small shark, then taking a photo of my father striding along the beach way in front of me with a huge cloud reaching into the sky over him. Most of all I remember the paintings on the island; I remember having to clamber over rocks and then walk up a hill and there being great vertical slabs of rock and having to walk through quite a narrow passage in between them to see the rock paintings and hand stencils, and asking permission to take photos.

In November 2009 I attended 'Barks, Birds and Billabongs', a conference at the National Museum of Australia on the fiftieth anniversary of the American–Australian scientific expedition to Arnhemland. The expedition had base camps at Groote Eylandt, Oenpelli and Milimgimbi. One of the conference convenors, Martin Thomas, had interviewed Gerry Blitner, who had helped the 1948 expedition just as he had helped my father. I took some photos from my 1973 trip which I had been looking for over many years and miraculously located and had printed about two weeks before the conference. At the conference I met five of Gerry's children, all of whom remembered me and my father visiting them and going out in Gerry's boat. Gerry died in 2008. His son Donnie Blitner was able to tell me the name of his boat and that indeed the island we visited was Chasm Island where today no-one is allowed to go.

Australia is part of Oceania, a place more sea than land. The word 'oceanic' means merging with the world. It is an idea which was incomprehensible to Sigmund Freud, though he mentioned its introduction to him by novelist Romain Roland in a letter in 1930 at the beginning of *Civilisation and its Discontents*:

It is a feeling which he [Roland] would like to call a sensation of 'eternity', a feeling of something limitless, unbounded — as it were 'oceanic'... it is a feeling of an indissoluble bond, of being one with the external world as a whole.

As a child in Austria I learnt a song the first line of which was *Weisst du wieviel Sternlein stehen an dem blauen Himmelszelt?* A literal translation reads: 'Do you know how many stars stand in the blue tent of the sky?' The song went on to ask other large questions such as: 'Do you know how many clouds travel the world, do you know how many grains of sand are on the beach, do you know how many fish are in the sea?' And so on. The answer contained in the song was 'God knows', not meant as in 'well, who knows' but in a comforting way to describe a reliable omnipotence. It said that He knows how many of them there are, and loves them all just like He knows and loves you. It was a song for children, after all. The song raises questions asked by all children of their parents in one way or another: 'who knows the world, is the world measurable, who made me, what is my place here, do I have to die, does anyone love me?'

July

The answer that God does is unsatisfying to many people and certainly was to me. To say that there is an invisible Father who will look after you, who acts mysteriously on your behalf was not comforting to me as a young child with a particularly erratically behaved father. It seemed to have the purpose of making me feel even more powerless and patronised, kept in ignorance of what was going on as if I was not capable of knowing the truth. Perhaps an acceptance of mystery as well as a feeling for the oceanic is at the bottom of all religious thought and faith – but I was not ready for such a thought at that time, nor was it ever presented to me like that.

My previous experience of God was in the suburb of Baldwin on Long Island in North America where my best friend Suzy went to Sunday School. I went along with her once and was immediately disillusioned when the first thing that we were asked to do was to put money in a collection plate. I thought that God should not be connected with money and if He was just a way to get money, even from small children, then I thought He was not deserving of my respect or attention. I never went back to Sunday School. I have to admit that I was haunted by the thought of a giant angry invisible foot, the foot of God, which might stand in my way as I walked to primary school. And perhaps a large invisible finger pointing down at me and a voice booming out: 'This girl thinks she can defy Me!' If the foot was invisible would it be made of something like glass? Would it be like a line drawing or would it be permeable? If I could walk through it then how would I know it was there? If I didn't know it was there then was it there at all? I was prepared to risk it.

Compared to religion art was free. It was free to enter galleries and walk and wander, free to look at works of art in spacious and peaceful places with shining floors where you decided how long you looked at something and did not need to sit still while someone talked endlessly as you fought to stay awake. Here were things made by people in other times and current times, objects from the recent past, the far distant past and the present, from all over the world. They did not ask to be paid but offered themselves freely. They were made by people and were there to communicate with other people. They were treasured and kept in special places, yet they had connections to what I might make myself or find at home either in books or on the wall. I wonder now how much I also responded with pleasure to the architecture of the museums and galleries, those expansive calm spaces with their large amounts of beautiful polished materials like marble, wood, metal and glass. I have an ongoing habit of appreciating the shiny floors of public buildings, and their impressive restrooms with their heavy doors, hi-tech taps and cutting edge bathroom fittings. It is an experience of the palatial which, like most people, I will never get anywhere else.

The artworks were accessible to me as objects the qualities of which I might come to know intimately without needing to own them. They seemed a lot less complicated than people, certainly they stayed still to be contemplated. If I owned something about them it was what they made me feel or think. New art was always being made everywhere in the world, thus endless discovery of it was possible. There was plenty of discovery involved too in looking at old art and finding out about it and developing a personal series of touchstones or making up my own mind about the works called masterpieces and deciding what I thought about them. Though I could become more and more informed about it my personal response was always an important part of the equation. In some way art belonged to me in the same way that it belonged to anyone who looked at it.

Immigrating from my birthplace Australia with my family in 1955 to America, thence to Austria in 1961 and back to

July

Australia in 1963, my early life took me repeatedly to live in countries starting with A. My bent against organised religion which began in America continued in Austria where in Grade Three I got special permission not to pray with all the others in class every morning. Sadly the girl I had to stand next to, a small demon called Brigitte with a short brown fringe and fat rosy cheeks, while everyone else had their eyes closed used to pinch my skinny little arm really hard in her rage at my ungodliness. Later and older in Adelaide I quietly conformed, and calmly prayed and hymned at a non-denominational school holding prayers and Bible readings every morning without either being a believer or needing to announce that I wasn't. Thus I heard readings, often the same pieces many times, from the King James Bible regularly over eight years and was filled with its language, rhythms, imagery and stories which I responded to as literature, mythology and poetry rather than religion. Any probing questions about religion or indeed literature infuriated my teachers, so I learnt to be silent about my doubts.

While in America and Austria, as a native-born Australian I knew enough to say where I came from when asked, however as I had left my birthplace in Melbourne when I was one year old I did not know for many years what it meant to be Australian, or even to be in Australia. Of course my grandmother sent us Vegemite, and there are photos and even a short reel of film of the first house I lived in that my mother and father built like many post-war young couples with the aid of their friends. It was located at Ringwood in Victoria and surrounded by bush. A feature of the house that the film especially dwells upon is the long dancing shadows of the gum trees on the white chimney.

Art became a kind of homeland for me beyond and between countries, a place where familiarity and knowledge could be built up, where pleasure could be found and curiosity stirred. It was the ideas and feelings that I collected through art by looking at books and visiting galleries and sites in America and Europe as a child that made it attractive to me.

I remember getting lost among the canals and bridges of Venice, watching hot glass being blown and stretched into horses, fish and vessels on the island of Murano, and in Pompeii being shocked and delighted by the roofless houses and the cobbled streets, and especially the painted walls with their rich colours and evocative textures. The ambience and idiosyncratic beauty, the sublimity and cultural complexity of these cities, the mystery and stubborn materiality of art present in them, rests in me like objects fixed at the bottom of a glass paperweight, magnified from some angles, diminished from others but always present as a foundation or base for everything that came afterwards.

Like any child I received fragments of stories and visions from my reading, my experience and my parents. In Yugoslavia where the roads were white dust and full of potholes we carried a whole smoked ham as a gift to relatives in the boot of the car, and my mother pointed out the bitter aloe trees which flower once before dying. When the car, an old Hillman Minx, broke down and had to be repaired in a village, we ate some of the ham sitting by the side of the road playing cards using the folding table and chairs we were also carrying as a gift. My father had a broken leg in plaster and would shout each time we drove over a bump. A little later he and my mother went to East Berlin and when the car broke down in the middle of the no-man's land between East and West he had to push the car dragging his broken leg behind him.

In Venice I saw the Bridge of Sighs over which the condemned would walk to their deaths. I was especially haunted by the bodies of a dog and of a woman who died during the eruption of Vesuvius and whose shapes were cast in plaster and placed in

July

the Pompeii Antiquarium. Plaster is an intensely evocative material — the luminous ground for all fresco paintings it delicately collects colours and impressions. Years later in Canberra Gillian Mann taught me to make plaster blocks as a printmaking surface, as developed in Poland when other materials were hard to get. Making plaster involves adding it as a fine powder in soft white handfuls to a bucket of water, judging the quantity required by both sight and feeling. Once it is mixed there is only a limited time to pour it before it goes hard. It goes through a chemical process a little bit like a miniature version of the creation of the world as it gives off heat while turning from a liquid into a solid. This is always very magical, silent and mysterious. Plaster is made from gypsum which was formed by deposits of salts in inland lakes over millions of years. When gypsum is ground to a fine powder and heated or calcined, three-quarters of its water content is lost, but when water is re-introduced, the mixture reverts to its original rock-like composition.

We made the journey from New York to London by ship, out past the Statue of Liberty and across the Atlantic to the White Cliffs of Dover, then after two years living in Austria, there was another journey by ship, this time from Europe to Australia, past the Rock of Gibraltar to Pompeii, then through the Suez Canal, seeing pyramids and camels, drinking cups of beef tea on the ship's deck and learning about Australia through colouring-in line drawings of flora and fauna. On each trip our luggage mysteriously vanished so that we had to buy new clothes on the ship or at ports. I remember having a new bathing suit of lettuce-green crimped cotton from the ship shop. While crossing the Equator I recall wearing this swimsuit on my spaghetti white body, being covered with melted pink ice cream, submerged and then carried fearful and tearful across the swimming pool by a sailor dressed as a mermaid.

AN OPENING

I had already nearly drowned while staying at Kolodeje nad Luznici in South Bohemia in Czechoslovakia with Alfred Radok and his family. We all swam down a river to go to the dairy to buy cheese, and as I couldn't swim I was placed in an old rubber tyre which flipped over almost drowning me. Alfred was a theatre director and had small models of theatres in his office on which he worked out how plays would be staged. My parents left us there while they went to Berlin. I was certain they were never coming back and remember embroidering handkerchiefs with cross-stitch (they had the designs printed on them in deep purple ink) and then washing the ink out in the sink at night while weeping – water attracts water.

When we arrived in Perth my sister and I wanted to know what was wrong with all the girls who were covered in brown spots, which we were quickly told were healthy freckles.

How do we learn about art, do we swallow whole the tales we are told, or do we make up our own minds? Does something always mean what the experts say it means or does it mean what you think it means? How do we decide what art is? How does our own history affect our approach to it? Is art for specialists, insiders and outsiders, or can its ideas be made accessible to all comers or popularised, as now happens with science? I believe that there must always be an element of openness in art and in its interpretation. This is vital to the place that it occupies in human life. It is a space against conformity, rigidity and convention, a space of possibility and discovery, invention and creativity – an ever-renewing starting point for the ongoing development of human culture.

In the mid-sixties I began to teach myself art stories. It involved a lot of reading and looking, at books, magazines and exhibitions, and making lists of names and movements, and learning to be able to tell one artist's work from another, a woodcut from an etching and an oil painting from a print, a watercolour from a drawing, and so on. The names and types of all the different media and being able to tell them one from another really fascinated me. Many art stories were about people and their lives, their struggles and successes, but most were about what they made, the images and objects that they brought into being, the residue of their lives. There was something addictive about art stories as they were both heroic and sad. Like all biographies they ended in death with unrelenting monotony, but something was left, something remained, that dragged that person into the next century and the next. The art spoke across time and culture. The stories were about ideas and individuals but also about societies, civilisations and the disappearance of civilisations, and most of all about material evidence of existence, evidence which intermingled the individual and the social, thought and feeling, craft and concept.

The study of art at secondary school had a peculiar licence about it, an intoxicating breath of freedom. The notion, a kind of jumbled suburban myth, was in the air that art could not be judged or taught. That people had judged it, and been found to be wrong, and since then no-one was prepared to be wrong in that way again. This meant that art could get away with anything. The artwork of Marcel Duchamp – the best-known example being a urinal that was first shown as a found object called *Fountain* in 1917 – and that of Andy Warhol – his Campbell's soup cans were first shown in 1962 – were daring, almost absurd examples of this 'anything goes', 'in your face', 'up yours' attitude. The indefinable slippery quality of art and its purported uselessness made it an apt place for experimentation and risk-taking. It was a place of looseness where definitions might burst their boundaries and multiply.

AN OPENING

I remember going to an exhibition opening somewhere in Adelaide in the late sixties where large open boxes of cigarettes sat invitingly on tables and glasses of sherry and wine were endlessly served with yellow cubes of cheddar cheese and Jatz crackers. These gifts seemed the height of generosity and something like an initiation rite. Giving is a mysterious part of the art experience. Mostly you do not pay to go to exhibitions, and when you go to exhibition openings you are given free drinks and often food. The symbolism of thus getting something for free has metaphoric connections to the freedom of visual art itself. The gift of art requires something back from us, not necessarily the buying of the work but the gift of time, thought and feeling involved in taking it into our lives. But we do not need to own it to get something precious from it. And though our interpretation of it may be different from that of other people it is equally right.

Notions of reciprocity and sharing lie at the basis of gift-giving. In Canada the custom of potlatch by the indigenous peoples on the Northwest Coast involved huge excessive feasts and gift-giving. Potlatches were banned by the British partly because they considered them a disruptive act against the idea of private property, for which all are meant to strive and which has at its base a need for inequality in order to engender competitiveness and envy. Yet rather than demonstrating a simple anti-materialism the sense of abundance and profligate generosity present in the potlatch is a working through of long-term relationships of reciprocity and status. The more that you give the greater is the debt owed to you. A version of this kind of relationship can be read into art which freely offers contemplation of ideas and materials, their transformation and placement, and the investment of time, thought and energy, by the artist. Being an 'Indian giver' in my childhood meant someone who took back what they had given. But the idea of a culture of sharing, to give away to

July

others what is given to you, to not store up material goods but to share them and thus to live in the moment, is at the heart of indigenous thinking all over the world. The setting up of intricate obligations and a sense of being embedded in relationships is not about a romantic sense of oneness but is about responsibility, and extends to the natural and non-material worlds.

When new ideas or technologies are introduced to indigenous communities they are often used in unpredictable and ingenious ways. Salvage anthropology got its name from the notion of saving/salvaging pieces, objects as well as concepts, of indigenous cultures shipwrecked on the shores of Western colonising cultures. The idea was that invaded cultures were pure and that their purity would be corrupted by encounters with the West. This would be followed by the commencement of an inevitable homogenising global journey for all peoples to become like the Western human, the ultimate link in an evolutionary chain of human development. But is global homogenisation of culture really inevitable or even likely? What if instead of 'rescuing' indigenous cultures we saw it the other way round – indigenous ideas being used in rescuing ways by non-indigenous cultures? And vice versa.

Bernard Smith's great book *European Vision and the South Pacific* shows how encounters with Australia and the Pacific influenced thought in the rest of the world, and ends with some words written by John Ruskin: 'If you can paint one leaf you can paint the world.' The sighting of unknown things on Pacific voyages in the nineteenth century introduced a lively freshness into the works of the artists recording them. Today we see the drawings and paintings that they made as both art and science. The world itself rather than any imagined place is freshly seen as extraordinary. There is ambiguity in Ruskin's statement about the leaf.

It can mean something moralistic as if to say: 'Well if you can be accurate in a small thing then you can be accurate in a big thing, and as your skills develop you will be able to make exact copies of all of the world and this is what knowledge is – coming to an understanding of the world by copying (replicating) it.' This is also one approach to art – a seizing of exact appearances in order to possess. Or Ruskin's statement can be read as having a wider meaning in which painting is a special way of understanding what surrounds you and thus involves another kind of knowledge than can be achieved merely by seeing. In this way of thinking the world is re-created by the creation of art and made more humanly intelligible by this re-creation.

Many indigenous artists make art with this in mind. It is part of their ancestral traditions to paint, draw and make ceremonial objects, and these activities mean participating in the generative forces and impulses which keep everything in the world moving. There is frequently no word in indigenous languages that translates directly as art. The word for design, sign, pattern or meaningful mark refers to the designs on birds and fish and trees, stones and water, the earth and the sky, as much as to the designs made by people. Thus there is equivalence rather than a separation between life forms. This embeds people and their activities in a world patterned with significance and meaning, to which they contribute and from which they learn.

The notion that everything in the world is made from variations of the same substance is common to contemporary science and to indigenous thought. The scales on a fish, the sparkle of the sun on water, the patterns on bark, feathers and lizards in their repetitive structures are signs of purpose and links to the Dreaming for Aboriginal people. Patterns that appear in Aboriginal art are shaped in imitation of such designs, though often reduced to a very minimal form. This abstraction and

July

reduction has the effect of making the designs like hieroglyphs or proto-writing, suggesting the letters of an alphabet written in the natural substances of the world. Yet each sign has many layers of meaning. A circle can be a camp, a breast, a waterhole or something else. Parallel lines may be rain, sandhills or clouds. Concepts of trans-substantiation, metamorphosis, transformation, interchangeability are all evoked by the multiple meaning of the designs. But thinking about the world through correspondences between things is not the same as thinking about measurement and asking how many fish are in the sea or how many stars are in the sky. Or is it?

The public purpose of Captain James Cook's journey to the Pacific in 1768 was to observe the Transit of Venus which he did from Tahiti in the specially built Fort Venus on 3 June 1769. Then he circumnavigated and mapped the coast of New Zealand before opening his secret instructions which asked him to look for the unknown south land Terra Australis Incognita.

> *You are likewise to observe the Genius, Temper, Disposition and Number of the Natives, if there be any, and endeavour by all proper means to cultivate a Friendship and Alliance with them, making them presents of such Trifles as they may Value, inviting them to Traffick, and Shewing them every kind of Civility and Regard; taking Care however not to suffer yourself to be surprized by them, but to be always on your guard against any Accident. You are also with the Consent of the Natives to take possession of Convenient Situations in the Country in the name of the King of Great Britain; or, if you find the Country uninhabited take Possession for his Majesty by setting up Proper Marks and inscriptions, as first discoverers and possessors ...*

Living in the north of Australia, Rembarranga man Paddy Fordham Wainburranga's story about Captain Cook as graphically seen in his paintings and in the 1988 film *Too Many Captain*

Cooks describes Cook as a figure who fought Satan and won, as well as bringing ceremony and lots of white man's possessions to the Aboriginal people in Australia. According to Wainburranga the original Captain Cook was not warlike but his sons, the many Captain Cooks, who came later with guns, killed many Aboriginal people and took over Australia, definitely were.

> *White people don't know Australia. We know Australia. We've known it from the early times, when the birds were human beings. Captain Cook from a million years ago. All the birds knew him. Captain Cook was a lawman like Adam and Eve. Captain Cook came from Mosquito Island to Sydney Harbor. Aborigines didn't have material things. Captain Cook had all material, white man's things. No one can change our law. No one can change our culture. Because we have ceremony from Captain Cook. This story is for all time. Nothing can change it.*

I first saw Wainburranga's paintings and the film in which he appears alongside paintings by Harry Wedge in the gallery at Tandanya National Aboriginal Cultural Institute in 1992. Wainburranga retold the story of Captain Cook while Wedge retold the story of Adam and Eve. Here is part of the long text that accompanies Harry Wedge's painting *Adam and Eve getting evicted.*

> *God told them that this garden is theirs all they have to do is stay away from that tree, but Eve like a woman is curious. She nagged at Adam to have a look at the tree. Adam said we were told to stay away from the tree but she ended up persuading Adam to have a look at the tree. When they went over to look they found a beautiful snake curled around the fruit tree. The snake said in a cool soft voice, 'Pick the fruit and have a taste.' As Eve went to stretch out her hand for the fruit Adam said 'no we are not meant to touch anything from this tree!' Then the snake said to Adam, 'Don't be a square' and Eve*

July

said to Adam, 'This fruit won't hurt us at all.' ... When Adam took a bite suddenly there was a big electrical storm then a big raving voice to tell them to fuck off out of the garden. Adam told Eve they had to leave the place and never return. As they were walking away Adam said to Eve, 'Are you fuckin' happy now?' Then Eve said to Adam, 'Don't start now.' They left and two dark people came into the garden as the garden was dying off. ... The beautiful snake said for them to have a taste of this last piece of fruit ... Then they started to look for something on the ground and the snake was getting curious and he asked them what they were looking for. One of them turned round and said: 'We are looking for a bundi, and we're going to bundi you and eat you and the snake said its time for me to cut out of here. As the snake was talking a big black beautiful spirit popped out of nowhere and frightened the two dark people and he said to them, 'This garden is your home for the rest of your generations to come.'

Both these stories diverge from the versions usually told. Their partisan and lateral perspectives surprised me and made me laugh out loud when I encountered them, as they boldly shifted around the stories I knew and demonstrated a few of the many possible ways of seeing and interpreting events. Not two ways but multiple ways, perhaps as many as there are stars in the sky.

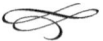

I bought the dog for one hundred dollars over the phone as a gift for my son on his thirteenth birthday. He was the runt of the litter and looked very small and shy next to his boisterous sisters. My son named him Skeeter after a character in a cartoon. Skeeter is mostly a Staffordshire terrier but his mother had blue heeler in her so he has a lot of hybrid vigour and a rich ancestry. Staffordshire terriers were bred in the UK from bulldogs, bull mastiffs and bull terriers to be hunting pig dogs sent in to pull the pig down at the last minute by grabbing it by the throat and not letting go. They were also used in dog fights. Contradictorily, as they are extra good with children they are also known as The Nanny Dog. Blue heelers were bred by Australians from cattle dogs and dingoes. They are known for stamina and intelligence. When we walk Skeeter and I are always linked by the lead as he is too unpredictable to be let off. He reads the ground fiercely and closely as if it is an old newspaper in a holiday house on a rainy day.

AUGUST
a new language

> *Really, a new language needs to be developed, an energetic and tellingly descriptive way of explaining this new art scenario ... a visual-emotional response; to engage the senses and the imagination and to counter the commonplace approach to art of this type with its overkill of didactic wall text.*
>
> Djon Mundine

In 1986 I hid two books from the National Gallery of Victoria bookshop under my coat and left the gallery with them. This was not something I usually did and my heart beat hard as I walked away but, though I had no money to buy them, I needed to have those books and I treasure them still. They are *Mr Sandman Bring Me a Dream* edited by Andrew Crocker and *The Face of the Centre: Papunya Tula Paintings 1971–1984* edited by Annemarie Brody. The first was published in 1981, the second in 1985. Curiously each book has the same image on its cover, a painting called *Tilpakan* (1980) by Turkey Tolson Tjupurrula – the entire image is on *The Face of the Centre* and the central detail of it on *Mr Sandman*. The painting is about the Dreaming journey of a poisonous brown snake who painted his body when he arrived at Tilpakan, the waterhole where he lives. Both books are full of the energy, freshness, wonder and sense of discovery and possibility that attended the initial blossoming of contemporary Aboriginal art in Australia in the late twentieth century when it was a new story. It is a story that has since been told many times and will continue to be told and retold. It is a story that is historical yet personal to each person who tells it. It is a story with multiple perspectives and starting points. I don't want to retell the story but to describe how it affected me, what it made me think and what a revelation it was. Though it is an overwhelming genre now, in the early 1980s contemporary Aboriginal art was just a glimmer on the horizon.

There is tremendous affection towards Aboriginal art and culture on the part of the countless people who think about it, talk about it or work with it. The artists are often charismatic characters, intense and powerful, with complex lives. The individual scholars, historians, anthropologists, curators, writers, art advisers and artists who are or have been involved with them are dedicated to them in a special way. Like anything involving love, Aboriginal art arouses great passion. There are many word-of-mouth apocryphal stories about the artists that circulate or that appear once and rarely again. Two examples took place at the National Gallery of Australia, one when Emily Kame Kngwarreye stopped in front of *Blue Poles* by Jackson Pollock, frowned, and on being asked what she thought, her response was that she was thinking about her favourite dog back at her camp who was unwell when she left. And upon seeing Mark Rothko's *Black, brown on maroon,* Rover Thomas said: 'Who's that bugger who paints like me?'

Many Western Desert paintings and artworks from other remote Aboriginal communities emanate great graphic energy and brilliance. Where does it come from, this vivid and dynamic power? Is the energy from the intensity of feeling that the painters have for their country? Is it ancestral power? Is it authenticity, or sincerity? Does it emanate from the country itself and the art translates those emanations into graphic signs? How do the works communicate the emotion that charges the best of them with such intensity?

These questions go to the heart of how any art communicates. Do we simply imagine the emotions of an artist or can they be conveyed through their work? How can we read an artist's sincerity and does it matter? Can it cross cultures and languages? How, in any case, do intangible qualities take on tangibility? In some way this is like asking how art works at all.

There has frequently been a defensive level around the discussion of Aboriginal art in Australia. People feel strongly about it and the depth of their feelings means that they sometimes wish to protect it and own the interpretation of it through their expertise in it. Or protect its makers. The issue of possession – possession of the truth and possession of permission to speak – are vital components in the debate. While some gatekeepers and experts are open to not caging the work behind their expertise and experience, there are others who want to cordon off Aboriginal art and culture. There are also Aboriginal people who want to place strong protocols around the work as if it differs from all other art. Can anyone talk about it? Is a new language required? Is exhaustive insider knowledge required? Can it be treated critically as art or, if authentically Aboriginal, is it all good? How do we define it, is it anything made by an Aboriginal person? Is Aboriginal culture the same as any other culture? Do 'they' have something that 'we' have lost, as many people have said? Did we ever have 'it'? Does Aboriginal culture join all cultures as an equal or must it be seen on different terms and treated differently? How do we communicate across cultures? Is it possible to assert or celebrate difference without creating hierarchies? When we look at Aboriginal art can we look directly at it or are we always looking at our idea of it? How much of culture is about rights, how much about responsibilities? Who decides? How are the valuable ideas of indigenous peoples from all over the world incorporated into other knowledge systems? Does incorporation mean assimilation? Do other knowledge systems need to change radically in order to be able to encompass indigenous thought? Can indigenous thought be encompassed by anyone who is not indigenous? Is indigenous thought owned by indigenous people? Is Western thought owned by Western people? Is ownership of thought possible?

All of these questions have swirled around inside my head for the last twenty or so years. It seems to me that indigenous cultures are not 'other' cultures to be studied, consumed and assimilated but are each an example of yet 'another' culture that contains messages about human connection to the earth as a necessary and primary basis to all culture. Aboriginal art demonstrates that the intellectual structures conceived by people are reflections of structures within the world and thus amount to a discourse of belonging and recognition, a discourse of love. All too often art is considered to be functionless and purposeless. The purpose of art, the function of art, is demonstrated by Aboriginal art, *to be able to be* about connection and location.

My experience of Aboriginal art began on Groote Eylandt in 1974 when I was shown rock art. This made me start looking for Aboriginal art when I started art school in Canberra eight years later. On looking up Aboriginal art in the art school library catalogue I found only two books, *Modern Australian Aboriginal Art* by Rex Battarbee and *Modern Aboriginal Paintings* by Rex and his wife Bernice, published respectively in 1951 and 1971.

Battarbee was a farmer who was injured in World War I and later studied commercial art but, as his entry in the *Australian Dictionary of Biography* says, 'developed a preference for the outdoor life of a landscape painter'. In 1932 he went to Central Australia to paint with a friend, John Gardner, in a T-Model Ford converted to a caravan. That year they showed their paintings at the Hermannsburg Lutheran mission, and again in 1934, the second time specifically to the Aboriginal people at the mission. They also painted portraits of Aboriginal people. At the 1934 exhibition Albert Namatjira asked how much money the artists would receive for their paintings. On learning how much they would fetch, possibly as much for one painting as he was getting for a year's work, he said 'I can do the same'. Returning in 1936 Battarbee taught watercolour techniques to Namatjira on a two-month painting trip on camels to Palm Valley and the MacDonnell Ranges. Namatjira went on to start a school of watercolour landscape painting among his countrymen, sell lots of his work and eventually meet Queen Elizabeth II. He became an Australian citizen, ironically the first Aboriginal person to receive this somewhat tainted honour, but was tragically not treated as one and was not allowed to lease grazing land, buy land or build a house in Alice Springs and, legally, had to treat members of his extended family as non-citizens. He died in 1959 but lives on in his work and as a pioneer of Aboriginal art.

In 2009 I visited Hermannsburg to see the place where Namatjira first saw Battarbee's paintings and to see the landscape for myself. Although it is a tourist destination the mission at Hermannsburg is not at all flash, but rather humble as if the past was just around the corner. The nineteenth century is still closely present in the blackboards simply painted on the walls of the schoolroom, the ancient trees, the red earth, the old whitewashed buildings with their thick stone walls in one of which original paintings by Namatjira and his relatives hang. These days it is said that the gifted Namatjira painted his country as authentically as any contemporary Aboriginal painter using traditional iconography, and a huge number of Aboriginal artists paint in his style, continuing to use Battarbee's very conventional method of watercolour painting as an Aboriginal art tradition.

After studying the paintings in Battarbee's two books my education in Aboriginal art continued in 1982 when I saw the extraordinary work made by the Wik people of Cape York, a series of ceremonial sculptures collected by Frederick McCarthy at Aurukun in 1962 that were on permanent show at the time at the Institute of Anatomy in Canberra. This wonderful collection was displayed inside a number of glass cases among other displays of Australian and Oceanic artefacts in a time warp, a crowded dim space with polished dark wooden floors and an elevated mezzanine level of rows and rows of books. When you pushed open the heavy wooden and glass door it triggered a sound tape so that tribal singing and music filled the room. The murky natural light, the vivid objects with their piercing eyes, the singing and droning all emphasised the presence of spirits and power. This striking Art Deco building built in 1930 (and whose designer and architect are, curiously, unknown) is today used as the National Film and Sound Archive. Throughout the building there are many Australian animal decorative motifs like glazed clay koala head rosettes, carved stone frill-necked lizard panels and a stained glass platypus skylight to make up what the Register of the National Estates has described as 'some of the finest examples of nationalistic Australian Art Deco design and detailing in Australia'. And in the foyer Phar Lap's great heart, looking bilious green in a big glass jar, was displayed next to a small jar containing the heart of an ordinary racehorse.

I arrived in Canberra in 1977 with a scholarship to do a

master's research degree at the ANU on the theme of the quest in Herman Melville's *Moby Dick*, Thomas Pynchon's *V* and Patrick White's *Voss*. At the time it was unusual to study either American or Australian literature let alone put them together. Even to be a woman in this atmosphere, though not unique, was odd. The cutting edge of reading was Roland Barthes's *Mythologies* and John Berger's *Ways of Seeing*, both of which I found dictatorial, unconvincing, dull and irritating. Barthes put me to sleep; I thought most of his comments were common sense, trivial or laboured rather than revolutionary, and while Berger's writing was lively I couldn't agree with what I saw as his authoritarian interpretations of 'our' responses to art. I did not feel included in his 'we'.

I had applied for several scholarships, desperate to leave home but not really knowing how. I was offered several but took the first one, which was at the ANU. I remember the application went to an office at Woden and I thought Canberra must be a mythic place if there was a suburb there named after a Norse god. I was also interested in the idea of Canberra's artificial lake, imagining it to be like a large handbasin, circular with a ceramic rim. One of the first things I did when I arrived was to look for the National Gallery of Australia. The guard on the steps of Parliament House pointed at an empty site near the lake and told me that was where it would be built.

The ANU humanities postgraduate students had offices in Childers Street in old prefab huts with no insulation, and the sight of dense dust motes and the smell of the heat-baked varnish of old yellow desks and brown lino comes back to haunt me when I think of them. A highlight was finding down the back of my desk an old poster of a Canaletto that had been nibbled quite hard by silverfish but still gave a sense of infinite horizon and belief in art that I needed so much in my tiny dusty enclosure.

His image of the pink brickwork of the Doge's Palace faded into white as if the light of the Venetian lagoon was dissolving it.

The year 1981 was one of miracles for me as I was fired from my job with the International Disasters Emergency Committee, found work with the National Campaign for Land Rights and Self Management in Queensland begun by Marcia Langton and others, helped run a conference for them and thus met and began to appreciate the great black humour of Aboriginal people who rather than being permanently made sad by suffering somehow found lots in the world to laugh about. I started a night class in etching at the Canberra School of Art which led to me getting into art school the following year, and I began a weekly radio program on the community radio station 2XX that I called *One World*, the exhilarating theme song of which was *We the people* by slide guitar legend Ellen McIlwaine. It begins with her saying the words 'And this song is for all of us because it's called we the people' followed by frenetic wordless singing and very rapid slide guitar playing.

One World focused on social justice and development issues and comprised interviews done on a portable tape recorder and then painstakingly edited back at the studio. The year 1981 was an amazing time to be in Canberra as the Third Congress of the World Council of Indigenous Peoples was held there in April. Indigenous people from all over the world attended; there were forums, dancing, singing, ceremonies and resolutions. It was a watershed experience, a delirious intoxication with justice and injustice, belief and conviction, knowledge, truth and the voice of the land, the earth. It seemed at the time as if indigenous people would at last become more and more part of the equation of daily life all over the world in both politics and culture. I took some words from a paper given at the conference and screen-printed them on a poster: 'If the transnationals and the colonialist governments continue to defy the natural order of things in their quest for material wealth, mother earth will retaliate, the whole environment will retaliate and the abusers will be eliminated. Things come back full circle, back to where they started. This is the prophecy of all indigenous peoples.'

In a twenty-first century world that overflows with countless examples of contemporary Aboriginal art, it is hard to imagine or describe the excitement that surrounded its emergence, which was of course different for everyone who experienced it. It came in various forms: in galleries, in calendars, in stamps, in cards, in films, in exhibitions and in books. It came as urban works and country works, political works and innovative works, works obviously closely tied to tradition and those dispensing with or transforming it. It came in bits and pieces, it came quietly, it often came with dancing and singing and ceremony, it came in intense exhibitions, in conversations, over months and years, building up momentum and excitement. It came in a series of revelations accompanied by interpretations and explanations. It came in the form of stories and ground paintings, singing and a strong sense of the ceremonial. And in a didactic way, as some of the purposes of art in Aboriginal communities and the protocols surrounding it were revealed; for example in Central Australia the complex notion of *kirda* and *kurdungurlu*, respectively owners and guardians of country, designs and Dreamings.

The inclusion of bark paintings by three artists, David Malangi, Djalambu Bungawuy and George Milpururr from Ramingining in Arnhem Land, in the 1979 *Biennale of Sydney* was a historic occasion. Their catalogue entry emphasised their professionalism as artists and their foreignness, their daily existence in another country lying within Australia, by saying that each was no stranger to warfare and had both taken and restored human life (suggesting magical abilities), that none could read or write a European language though each spoke three to nine languages, and that the paintings expressed their spiritual connection to their country and totemic responsibilities to the land and all it contains. It also said: 'The painters' only wish is that the Europeans who view their work will look far enough into the dreaming to find a starting point for real dialogue.'

As part of the 1982 *Biennale of Sydney* Aboriginal art was seen by a big public as a performative event when Warlpiri people from Lajamanu made, sang and danced an untitled large sand sculpture inside the Art Gallery of New South Wales in one of its internal courts. The large six by three metre groundwork drawn from public sacred ritual cycles was made of earth, red and white ochres and white plant down. The Biennale's subtitle was *Vision in Disbelief*, and I remember looking down from the balcony watching the performance holding my breath and feeling both incredulous and privileged to be able to see an ancient ritual from the centre of Australia in the middle of Sydney.

In November that same year in Canberra the first Rom ceremony to be performed outside Arnhem Land was held at the Australian Institute of Aboriginal Studies. Performed by the Anbarra people over four days the ceremony involved painting up, singing and dancing, and the presentation of ceremonial poles, one representing wild honey and the tail of stingray, and the other the morning star, masked plover and butterfly. The word Rom may be translated as indigenous knowledge, and is also the name of a ritual bringing reconciliation after a separation. As explained by anthropologist Ian Hughes:

Rom does not frame historical experience as progressively unfolding development, but as the working out of an unchanging law known as the Dreaming, which puts opposed or separated elements into mutual interdependence. Rom emphasises mutual interdependence and adaptation. Unlike Western notions of individuality, Yolngu knowledge is expressed in terms of complementary pairs which come into interdependent relationships, like the salt water and fresh water which mix at a particular place in the river.

I remember sitting on the grass waiting and watching and listening, and as with the dances performed during the World Council of Indigenous People's conference noticing how the long preparations, the consultations, the quiet times before the performances were as important as the performances themselves, which were over all too quickly.

Over the next few years not Aboriginal art in general but several individual works made by Aboriginal artists made a strong impression on me. In 1983, very large and spectacular Western Desert paintings were hung in the tall angular gallery at the end of a ramp in the centre of the National Gallery of Australia (NGA), which finally opened in 1982. Especially I recall Johnny Warangkula Tjupurrula's *Yala, Wild Potato Dreaming* painted in 1981. Its many yellow ochre concentric circles linked with double lines over a white dotted ground over patches of a range of shades of fine brown ochre marks in paint so thin that it seemed merely to stain the canvas rather than placing a layer of paint over it, were both hypnotic and astonishing. Asserting a closeness to and knowledge of the earth, and the presence of secrets in the form of mysterious mythologies and stories deep in the heart of the continent, the palpable energy and confidence emanating from the work was amazing. Around this time I also recall seeing Mick Wallangkarri Tjakamarra's *Old Man's Dreaming on Death or Destiny* painted in 1972. It was also a revelation. Its thin black, pink, yellow and white paint leaps from the flat surface of the board to vibrate in front of your eyes. I can read its symbols to the extent of seeing that it shows two men sitting in windbreaks with their shields near them. A U-shape is the shape people leave on soft ground after sitting on it and a bough shelter is also like a U. When I first saw this painting I looked around for more information and saw only its title, which was full of import as so little art claims to be about something as important and everyday as an old person thinking about death or indeed destiny. I thought then that one reason this art is valuable is because it is not about art but about life.

In 1984 Aboriginal art was on show at the Adelaide Festival in the form of vast canvases displayed in the single room of the nineteenth-century sky-lit gallery belonging to the Royal Society of South Australian Artists on the corner of Kintore Avenue and North Terrace. I was in Adelaide only very briefly and the gallery was closed when I got there, so I had to press my face up to the gap between the two heavy wooden gallery doors to glimpse a slice of it. What I saw – a fragment of a show called *Painters of the Western Desert: Clifford Possum Tjapaltjarri, Uta Uta Tjangala and Paddy Carrol Jungarai*, curated by Tony Bishop – made me catch my breath, it was so electric and glowing; the huge paintings pulsated with colour and crackled with energy. They were intensely optical and literally vibrated. The optical physiological power of paint has the potential to imitate the power implicit in, well, everything. The animism in me responded to the works, and while interested in the stories I still don't think that exhaustive knowledge of them is vital or maybe even achievable: it is the feeling they convey to the senses and the heart that is most important. Something is present and something is transmitted by colour, shape and texture, and this is the power of the work. Its vividness, its truth to the vividness of nature, to the nature of perception, is cross-cultural – or does it travel beneath culture? If we think of visual art as something that though it may include words and explanations is also something fundamentally without words then the languages of texture and of colour, of shape, structure and style of mark, are highly significant, not to show technique but to communicate and to emulate sensation, to return us anew to the vividness of being alive.

Yet another momentous exhibition was *Dreamings: The Art of Aboriginal Australia* exhibition, first shown in New York in 1988 at the Asia Society Galleries, then in Chicago and Melbourne in 1989, and in 1990 at the South Australian Museum. The works ranged over the country and over a wide time scale showing work from as early as possible and as late as possible. One work in particular stood out for me. It was a bark painting by a Tiwi artist based on Melville Island called Big Tom. The word Tiwi means 'human beings'. *Sun Woman at Wurriyupi* (1954) is the title of the work and in it the progress of the sun across the sky is shown. But I looked at the work before reading its accompanying wall label and saw a vertical row of four black discs, a quite large one at the bottom then a smaller one and then a very small one and then a larger one, all surrounded by upward streaming lozenges in yellow and red ochre. I decided that it must be showing the sun throughout a day as it looks big when it is near the horizon and small when it is high in the sky then bigger again as it sets. Subsequently finding out the title of the work was very satisfying, as I had guessed what it was about on the basis of my own experience. The colours in the work are very alive, particularly the yellow and its soft glowing luminescence.

In 1989 the National Aboriginal Cultural Institute Tandanya opened in Adelaide, and in 1990 held an exhibition called *East to West* in which the mapping purposes of Western Desert paintings were emphasised as the artworks were laid out by compass directions to resemble the topography of where they were made. It included crayon drawings on brown paper made by Aboriginal people at Mount Liebig in 1932 as well as the very latest acrylic paintings. Here I first saw Turkey Tolson Tjupurrula's very articulate painting *Straightening Spears at Illyingaungau* (1990),

AN OPENING

a work full of the presence of remembering or memory, and an experience of sand and sun, and shadow and blinding light, and wind and human presence. The activity, of straightening spears, has many layers of experience and implications in it, including memories for the artist and those looking at the work who know the activity. The painting uses variations of two colours of acrylic paint, a yellow ochre and a red ochre. They are painted over a black ground. Rather than being evenly hued there are variations in the density and application of the paint so that we seem to be almost looking through venetian blinds at something shadowy on the other side. Neither colour is particularly lighter or darker than the other one. Neither is positive or negative, but each is both, each recedes and comes forward. This balance between the colours makes them sit on the surface of the painting at the same time as they imply vast space. There is a strong charge of memory in the work. It is possible to think of the horizontal lines made of yellow dots joined together crossing the canvas as the lines made in sand by wind. It is also possible to think of them as the long lines of spears being straightened. Or to see in the shifting parts of the horizontal lines some shadows of people on the ground or their bodies in between you and the sun. There is a notion of squinting, of long shadows stretching over the ground and the shadows changing as the light changes. The painting flows between an evocation of a day, a camp, an activity, a place in the desert and the notion of straightening, of positive and negative forces coming into some sort of balance, of scale and the relationship of the body to the painting. The work is also about its materials or materiality. There is no attempt in the painting to make something regular and even, rather the dippings and re-dippings of paint and brush, the thickness of the paint when the brush is full and its thinness when it is running dry, all these small 'errors' or slips are integral to the work. This handmade irregularity of the work enlivens it and suggests an acceptance of the warts of life and hence its multifaceted character. The painting is not trying to create an ideal seamless world in art but rather something reflecting and hand in hand with a kind of pragmatism. Turkey Tolson made many other paintings on this subject but only this one has such charge and presence, the sense of shadowed figures in an environment of shifting air and light.

In E.H. Gombrich's most famous book *The Story of Art*, which my mother gave me in 1970, Australia is represented only by a photograph entitled 'Australian native, drawing a totemic opossum pattern on a rock'. This opossum pattern is not very different from those made on paintings on boards or canvas today by Western Desert Aboriginal artists. Gombrich uses the photo as a punctuation point, the last image and final moment of his first chapter which is called 'Strange Beginnings'. A new, albeit posthumous, version of his *Story* might place an opossum pattern or something very like it at the end of the book, thus sandwiching *The Story of Art* with Aboriginal art, taking us from the beginnings of art to today. Gombrich does not mention the opossum painting directly but says in reference to it that 'image-making in ... early civilisations was not only connected with magic and religion but was also the first form of writing ... if we want to understand the story of art we do well to remember, once in a while, that pictures and letters are really blood-relations'. This comment connects with the analysis of Aboriginal painting made by Geoffrey Bardon, the schoolteacher who encouraged the contemporary Western Desert painting movement in 1971 at the settlement of Papunya in Central Australia. Bardon described the works being made by Anmatyerre, Arrernte, Luritja, Pintupi and Warlpiri men as proto-writing. His first book on their work, *Aboriginal Art of the Western Desert* (1979), described the sign system used by the artists and gave translations of the signs.

Bardon emphasised the haptic level of communication involved in the paintings and how the artists would stroke and sing the painted shapes and lines. Indeed the early works look soft, as if they have been stroked. He wrote: 'The painters seemed to me to understand space as an emotional idea.'

Talking about Western Desert paintings in terms of their symbolic meanings, and interpreting their forms as the signs in a pictorial alphabet, is only one way of responding to them. As well as translating them into maps and diagrams it is possible to respond to them on an experiential level, joining your own experience of the earth, your knowledge about weather, landforms, plants, animals and life, to your experience of art, your acquaintance with and responses to paint and patterns, texture, colour, drawing and surfaces. Appreciation of the paintings is enhanced by increased knowledge about their languages, and about the lives and purposes of the artists, yet the works also speak directly and ask viewers to draw on what they already know about the world. About the way cloud patterns resemble patterns on bark or how a brush begins by being full of paint and gradually runs out of it.

In 1991 Geoffrey Bardon's brother James published an extraordinary but difficult novel called *Revolution by Night, or, Katjala wananu (The Son after the Father)*. The book foregrounds itself as 'a rough transcription of notes from a Professor Jack Dutruc, a survivor of the Wilier massacres'. The writing is dreamlike without much punctuation. The story is fictional but embedded in facts. Reading it is like being in a sandstorm where moments of clarity are replaced by swirling fog. It lifts the reader into a strange place where ideas are formed and brought to the surface only to slide away. The novel draws on the explorer Charles Sturt's experiences in his explorations in Australia from 1828 to 1844. It joins the language, often described as purgatorial, in Sturt's *Journal*, which combines his record of exploration with his intense religious feelings on entering unknown deserts and strange places, with speculations about the formation of Aboriginal culture and religion as they arose out of those very same places and conditions. It is very much an imaginative stream of consciousness rather than an anthropological approach to the complex and ultimately unknowable genesis of any human culture.

In keeping with its semi-documentary style and in the tradition of the novel that has been 'found' by the writer, *Revolution by Night* finishes with several appendices. They include an essay by Dutruc about Aboriginal art in which he claims that the paintings made at Papunya are simultaneously representations and embodiments of matter; and that they achieve four-dimensionality by incorporating a sense of space expanding in all directions at once. He calls them a system of 'eidetic recall' in which the artists 'see' the journeys that they recount. Eidetic images are vivid memory images which are viewed by those who see them like actual palpable pictures hanging in front of them. To think about art in the way described by James Bardon means understanding it as a physiological stimulus as well as a conceptual tool. It shows that art possesses a role that is forceful and physical, to be used both for thinking and remembering.

Dreamings, a key term used when explaining Aboriginal cosmology, was coined for this purpose in the late nineteenth century by Frank Gillen, postmaster of the Alice Springs telegraph station and enthusiast for Aboriginal culture. First it was Dream Time, which shifted into Dreaming and then Dreamings. Gillen was looking for a word to translate into English the Arrernte word *Alterrenge*. It is strange how it came about because though the word for dream in Arrernte is similar in sound, a homophone, to the word *Alterrenge*, this is not the case in most other Aboriginal languages, though they have a term with a meaning similar to *Alterrenge*. *Jukurrpa* is the Warlpiri word and rather than being called Dreaming it is often translated as 'the Law'.

The word Dreamings has become part of the Australian vernacular, and is used lightly by many people. It is often used in the media and advertising as a synonym for belonging and/or desire, even while maintaining its connection to Aboriginal culture. It possesses the flexibility of a hybrid concept and has developed through translation and mistranslation. Yet the full meaning of it is probably not really clear to many people. Dreamings are not considered mythology or metaphor by the Aboriginal people to whom they belong, but a true account of what happened when the world was created. Dreamings are creation figures and include everything and everytime, from landforms to trees, animals to diseases. They are both handed down and found, they belong to people and relate to things and places but also to events. They are in the past but also in the present. Aboriginal guidelines for living are set out by some Dreaming stories. Yet rather than being Just-So stories or only the setting-out of moral codes that the term 'the Law' suggests, it is the case that often in the stories all sorts of apparently random and arbitrary events take place along with the creation of the land and its people, its flora and fauna, often with love stories and sexual misbehaviour involved. This makes them a bit more like stories about Greek and Roman gods than Bible stories (though the Bible has its share of such events).

Dreamings link the past and the present and are also ongoing. Dreamings made something happen in the beginning, they still make something happen and they belong to or are in people living today as they were in people living in the past. Dreamings may be in a painting. Dreamings emphasise continuity and location, and the power of narrative to bring memory and place together. W.E.H. Stanner, an anthropologist who thought and wrote a lot about Aboriginal religion, thought that a better word than Dreamings would be 'Everywhen' thus linking place and time with a sense of eternity, infinity and ubiquitous power. Stanner also offers a sense of it as a life force. It was described to him by an Aboriginal man as: 'Like engine, like power, plenty of power: it does hard-work; it *pushes*.' Anthropologist Peter Sutton describes it in the words of Peter Peemuggina from Cape York as '*Epam epama*' — literally 'nothing is nothing', everything means something. In a conversation recorded for the Wagilag Sisters exhibition it was described by Yolngu man Don Gumana as like telecommunications: 'They're passing over each other, they're passing away back, they're passing through one another, same way, all Wititj (olive python), they're passing a message over one another. It's like a Telecom. It's like a Telecom.' Embedded in them is not necessarily a panacea, a key or a secret but something vital, the power of stories.

A few of the early Papunya paintings showed ceremonial costumes and regalia and resemble illustrations from encyclopedias or ethnographic books. However most of the works are designs which are not illustrations of culture but direct expressions of that culture. They are manifestations of ancestral power. The powerful optical effects present in many of them, such as the Tingari cycle paintings, in which concentric circles pulse and waver, demonstrate knowledge of organic patterns derived from close observation of nature and an understanding of human susceptibility to the repetition of certain forms.

When they found out what was happening at Papunya there was controversy amongst other Aboriginal people in the Western Desert region about whether these designs ought to be painted for public display and sale. The first exhibition of the paintings held at Alice Springs in 1974 was stoned by Aboriginal people in protest at the paintings' rumoured disclosure of secret-sacred designs, which they also owned. Surrounding communities continued to perceive the Western Desert painters as cultural delinquents well into the 1980s, according to historian Vivien Johnson's account. This was eventually resolved and now a huge and ever-increasing number of Aboriginal communities all over Australia make art for sale. The financial success of the Papunya artists showed that there was income to be made from art, which neither diluted nor diminished the power of the ancestors but actually raised its status through being visible and valuable in the wider world. This success also made it possible for people to buy Toyotas (Toyota Dreaming) to visit their Dreaming sites and to support their repatriation to their own country in outstations to extend and affirm traditional culture, and to avoid mainstream Australian life. Thus tradition was able to display flexibility and as Clifford Possum's brother Tim Leura Tjapaltjarri said to Geoff Bardon in reference to the culture providing for its people in this way: 'The money belongs to the ancestors.'

The Papunya paintings are based on ancient designs for the ground, the body and objects, designs that are modified and transformed by the materials with which they are made. In the very beginning the artists used ground ochres, house paint or poster paints mixed with PVA glue to make a fragile watery painting medium just like we did at school. The supports for paintings, which were primed black like skin or red like the earth, were, in the beginning, just pieces of masonite or composition board, old pieces of wood left over from building, or even tiles. In the early days the enthusiasm and urgency of the painters saw them paint eagerly on these makeshift supports. The poverty of means of these vivid works, their irregular shapes, thin paint and urgent marks gives them enormous *gravitas*, and a sense of necessity. Canvas and acrylic paints were introduced at the end of 1972 partly because canvases could be rolled up for storage and bigger works would not be so heavy.

In the work of several artists painting at Papunya in the early days of 1971, there are clear responses to painting on a hard surface, which is so different from painting on a body, on three-dimensional objects or on the ground. The especially radiant *Water Dreaming* (1972), a painting made by Johnny Warangkula Tjupurrula which, in many tiny dots and thin lines, stoppings and startings of white lines and yellow lines, over red and pink patches and lines, creates a veritable festival of water around a U-shaped symbol of a man sitting in a cave, is a good example. Such fine layered painting feats are sustained developments from ground or body paintings rather than reproductions or copies of them. They exploit the hard surface, the quick-drying paint and the fine work possible with the new media. They are a new language of art. And they are responses to what the artist has seen and knows.

As Bardon pointed out: 'Contrary to popular belief it often rains in central Australia and on this western desert. Aboriginal mythology concerning the spectacular effects of rain and hail in the desert, and the waterholes that survive in dry times, are profoundly lyrical.' And the year the painters began working, in 1971, in Central Australia there was much rain and normally dry rivers were twenty-four kilometres wide.

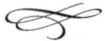

In Michael Perry Reserve where Second Creek runs through a series of small waterfalls into a large pool of water I sometimes fulfil my craving for seeing tadpoles. Here are growing a great

AN OPENING

range of trees: Bunya Bunya pines from Queensland, palms from all over the world, pines from many nations, and right at the top, on the other side of a cyclone fence dividing the park from the quarry where the hill is blasted, dug and taken away in trucks as quartzite sand, an immense oak tree. As South Australia began to be settled by Europeans in 1836 it can only have been there for about 170 years, but it looks really ancient. This area, the foothills to the east of the city, has five creeks running down as tributaries to the River Torrens. The plantings along and around the creeks of avenues of trees, of palms and bamboos, sometimes even now suggest the fertile valley of the Nile, a place where water makes possible an oasis of strong green growth, and the creation of gardens draws together all the countries of the world in their flora.

The dog rushes into the reeds at the edge of the pool and brings out a pale blue duck egg in his mouth. It is cold and must have been abandoned some time ago. He is very proud of his find and as I crouch down to study it we exchange bemused glances.

SEPTEMBER

written on the skin

The real leap *consists in introducing invention into existence.*
Franz Fanon

When Ah Xian won the National Sculpture Prize in 2001 with *Human human – lotus, cloisonné figure 1* (2000–01), a life-size female figure covered with cloisonné, I tore the image of the sculpture from the newspaper and put it on the side of the fridge where it stayed for years, as I found it so intensely mesmeric and fascinating. A human figure covered in pattern like a fully tattooed or painted body has a particular resonance in part because it echoes the cultures of people who wore or wear no clothes. It has a link to first things, it emphasises our essential nakedness by drawing attention to our skin. It has associations with magical transformations and metamorphoses. It is like a ghost or a spirit figure exactly human in its dimensions. The body is asserted as a canvas or blank page and drawn into a wordless communion with the rest of the world like poetry in which a hand possesses the tension of a leaf, a mouth opens like a flower.

Cloisonné is a highly sophisticated technique first devised in the Near East and introduced to China by skilled craftsmen fleeing Constantinople in 1453. It involves the creation of a design on a three-dimensional metal form with a lattice of thin walls of metal, often copper. Powdered coloured glass called frit is packed into the spaces of the design formed by the lattice, the whole piece is then fired in a kiln at a high temperature and the glass powder melts and turns into vitreous (glass) enamel. Several layers of frit and several firings may be necessary to totally fill the spaces between the wire. Then the whole is ground smooth and the exposed metal is lightly electroplated with gold. For many centuries cloisonné has been associated with China, though the first known examples of it were found in Cyprus around the twelfth century BC. In the purity of its opaque colours and its smoothness it resembles polished semi-precious stones and the exquisite feathers of birds, the wings of butterflies or the petals of flowers.

A few years before I saw *Human human* on my first trip away from my son when he was eight, I bought some pieces of cloisonné for him and for my mother at a shop in Chinatown in Sydney. Those two small objects are in front of me now, a blue and pink egg that hangs in the window and a mostly turquoise container about the size of a small apple; both are covered in flowers in an ecstasy of intricate decoration. On that same trip to Chinatown I also recall eating a clear fragrant soup full of semi-transparent wontons with pink prawns nestling inside them which gently brought me back to life when I was exhausted and lonely.

Human human was made by Ah Xian in collaboration with traditional craftspeople at the Jingdong Cloisonné Factory in Hebei Province, east of Beijing. Production of this large work was a lengthy, labour-intensive process; three sculptures were attempted and only one survived the process. At the beginning of his career in China Ah Xian painted nudes, a controversial choice considered pornographic and morally corrupt in China at the time. He first came to Australia as a visiting scholar in

September

1989. After witnessing the Tiananmen Square massacre in June 1989 he sought political asylum in Australia in 1990 and turned his concern with the human figure into three dimensions by making first plaster then porcelain busts painted with traditional Chinese designs at the Sydney College of the Arts. Later he was able to work with Chinese craftsmen at the Jingdezhen Porcelain Sculpture Factory in 1996 and in 1999. I first saw the series of porcelain busts called *China China* in Brisbane at an *Asia-Pacific Triennale* in 1999. Their combination of ancient hand-painted designs speaking of refined sensibilities and connoisseurship with actual human faces, mostly Chinese, brimming with vulnerability and thus somehow a vivid sense of the complex past of their country, is striking. In one way they are like living people embalmed in their culture, their mouths and eyes are sealed as if removed from connection with the outside world. In another way they are like beautiful chrysalises waiting for the right moment to emerge.

The female figure of *Human human* is decorated in a traditional overall pattern of tiny white and gold cloud shapes over which pink and white lotus flowers and veined green lotus leaves are twined. The fading of the colours from pink to white on the petals of the lotus, from dark green to light green on the lotus leaves, is especially lovely. The lotus is one of Buddhism's most significant symbols. It is customarily celebrated as a symbol of enlightenment, purity and a sign of hope in the journey towards enlightenment. The roots of the lotus are in the mud but its flowers rise above the water, a simile for the progress of the soul. As with Ah Xian's busts, the decoration covers all of the body with no special attention to the eyes or the ears, the mouth or the nose, but simply treats all of it as a shape, a vessel, to be covered. The effect of muteness that is thus created has a peculiar eloquence. Because her eyes are closed and all her senses are covered the *Human human* figure appears to be meditating, to be folded inside herself. At once a decorative object and reminiscent of a religious figure like a Buddha, she belongs to a world of contemplation and reverie yet is very human in her shape and demeanour.

Ah Xian makes casts of the bodies of his models in plaster before handing them over to the workmen who do the cloisonné or other processes. His models need to find great calm within themselves for the demanding task of having their bodies cast. In such a process the naked body is covered with a release substance like vaseline, straws are inserted in the nose, wax in the ears, the eyes and mouth are held firmly closed while multiple layers of plaster-soaked bandages are wrapped around the body. Because they are cast the figures are not idealised but hold on to small imperfections and variabilities, thus emphasising human vulnerability, frailty and individuality. There is an echo in them of the life-size terracotta warriors buried with the Emperor of Qin in 210–209 BC, each of which is different by virtue of having an individual head and hands.

Both ancient Greek sculpture and the work of Michelangelo and Rodin are evoked by Ah Xian's work as sculpture focusing on the naked human body, yet the pattern totally covering *Human human*'s surface marks it as connecting with a decorative art tradition rather than a figurative one – it is the combination of them that makes it powerful. In 1877 because of the lifelikeness of his work, its verisimilitude to skin and flesh, Rodin was accused of *surmoulage*, casting from a body rather than carving his plaster sculpture *The Age of Bronze*. Ah Xian does use *surmoulage*; his artistry is not so much in the making of the work, he did not carve or model the body, he does not make plaster, clay or marble take on the form and texture of living skin like Rodin did. His skill is in the casting and the concept but also

September

in commissioning the right traditional people to make his art. Thus his negotiating skills are present in the work, the skills of a Chinese person living in Australia getting Chinese craftspeople in China to create artworks which bring together Chinese and European art traditions.

Each culture that comes to Australia brings along its own customs and ways of doing things. Sometimes new ones are invented. Sometimes traditions which keep changing in the homeland, the 'Old Country', become rigid here as it is in that form that they represent connection to the past. This is most noticeable in language where the dialects brought over and taught to grandchildren are considered archaic and extraordinary in their place of origin. Artworks that tap into customary or traditional knowledge can renew or recreate the past. The experience of exile, of moving, of being a foreigner, of strangeness, is the flip side of a deeper understanding of what belonging and familiarity mean.

Sharing food, the open hand of welcome and hospitality, is universal human behaviour, but has different levels of elaboration in different cultures. The acts of cooking have great emotional resonance. A video by Paloma Ramos shows her Spanish mother making paella and tapas. The work is filmed in the kitchen, the centre of the home, the place of secret and unwritten recipes, time-worn movements, the sacraments of herbs and wine, of talk and method, aroma and vision, where all the senses of smell and touch, taste and hearing are paramount. A woman's hands move over a frying pan and she speaks incessantly in her own language. There are no subtitles and it is a chaotic scenario quite unlike a cooking program. The woman's face is not visible. Steam rises in front of the camera. The voice is muffled and the camera goes in too close to see what is happening, yet an immense sense of rhythm and of ritual is conveyed so that even as you watch with initial impatience there is a crucial shift of recognition, of familiarity and acceptance after which you are happy to stay on in this kitchen and let the video play over you, even if it is not clear what is happening. It is mesmeric and comforting, seductive and illuminating. Next to the video Ramos hung a wreath made of bay leaves and a bowl of red wine beneath a collection of light bulbs with crosses inside them. The light bulbs hang on the wall like a plait of garlic cloves warding off vampires.

A second-generation migrant, Bette Mifsud grew up on a market garden in New South Wales. Her photographic series *The Living Room* shows fragments of rural Australia – naked hills, a sole tree in a bare paddock, the artificial border created by a barbed-wire fenceline where stock have been kept out and masses of weeds have greened a field which sits hard against an acreage of dry yellow stubble, a dam sitting in the elbow of a tufty rocky hillside, a dry straw-coloured featureless hill stretching like a giant shoulder behind a house crouched among dark trees. Though completely unpicturesque the photos possess an immense emotional weight and are, in their emptiness, like vessels for feelings.

Stories of migration begin with home before they talk about homelessness. They circle around translation and broken language. The recurring presence in Australian art of stories of exile and migration, cross-cultural journeys and the creation of home in the midst of strangeness is an important part of a country where the question of origin is a constant. 'Where do you come from?', 'Where did your parents come from?', 'Why did they come here?' are everyday questions in Australia, no matter what you look like. It is almost a game, to guess, to tease, to fabricate, to draw out the final moment of identification and classification. Any appearance can hold a surprise, almost nothing is certain. Everyone knows that we all came not that long ago from somewhere else, except the indigenous, and often they have ancestors from other countries. We know that we are all somehow linked to some other place or places. And that often we are made of complex and exotic comminglings and couplings which make unexpected connections between Australia and other countries in the world. Yet many of these connections are not based on direct experience, but on stories and objects, photos and rituals, imagination and dreams. The view from Australia of other places is loaded with evocative words, sights and symbols. Sometimes they are misreadings that lend us the ability to cross cultures creatively on an everyday basis and, indeed, to move into the space between them which is not only a transit zone but a new place.

Do you need to experience homelessness to be able to empathise with others or can you learn it through your imagination? Some identities are more complicated than others; some people have very little to identify with. In secondary school English one of our books was *The Prussian Officer and other stories* by D.H. Lawrence. As my father came from East Prussia, a place that no-one knew much about and that no longer existed as it became part of Russia after the Second World War, some of my classmates at least briefly called me The Prussian Officer. Was I really that bossy? What comes to mind as a national characteristic of a Prussian? Apart from Bismarck and militarism, the two most significant and well-known people connected to the capital of East Prussia, Königsberg (now Kaliningrad), where my father was born, are Immanuel Kant and Käthe Kollwitz.

Kant, world-renowned philosopher, spent his entire life in and around his hometown, never travelling more than a hundred miles from Königsberg thus showing that travel may not be necessary for a broad or celebrated mind. His father, Johann Georg Kant, was a German craftsman, while his mother, Anna

AN OPENING

Regina Porter, born in Nuremberg, was the daughter of a Scottish saddle/harness maker.

Kollwitz, who lived a lot of her life in Berlin, made intense and forceful drawings and prints about love and grief, war and hunger. She is considered by many to be one of the greatest printmakers of all time. She was born in Königsberg. Her father, Karl Schmidt, was a radical Social Democrat who became a mason and housebuilder. Her mother, Katherina Schmidt, was the daughter of Julius Rupp, a Lutheran pastor who was expelled from the official State Church and founded an independent congregation.

The third well-known thing about Königsberg starting with k, are Königsberger Klopse, meatballs in white sauce with capers.

The whole question of nationality and where it comes from, how it is invented, discovered and passed on, is endlessly complex. For every person with a solid trail of ancestors there is one with a broken string. My father escaped from Germany to England in 1939 after the Reichskristallnacht to avoid going to a concentration camp like other Radoks who went to Theresienstadt, a ghetto and transit camp for Auschwitz. In 1940 with two of his older brothers he arrived in Australia on the *Dunera* along with other refugees, many of whom went on to be influential people in Australia and elsewhere. He would always say that he hated Germans, yet German was his mother tongue and Germany his homeland. His father's family was Jewish though not orthodox. His mother was German and named him Rainer Maria after the poet Rilke. My paternal grandparents were always known as Ranee and Rajah because of the honeymoon they took in Africa in 1913, from which I still possess the souvenir of three bristles from an elephant's tail plaited together. Along with my father's sister his parents eventually escaped from Germany and via the US ended up living in Melbourne.

September

My mother's family was a mixture of Scottish, British and Irish. Her father was Irish but her mother left him in 1920, leaving behind a one-year-old daughter Peggy but taking my two-year-old mother with her. Forever after Gladys would voice her hatred of the Irish, or so my mother told me. They went to live in the Mallee after Gladys married a dentist. My mother only found out she had a sister when she was in her fifties. (As we never lived in the same city I remember only a little about Gladys. She took us to see *The Sound of Music* at the palatial Forum Cinema in Adelaide, introduced me to the delights of drinking tea and bought us Fruchocs at the movies. The one saying handed down to me by my mother from Gladys is: 'Never do any housework after twelve noon.' After she died and I asked what she left me my mother said it was a small aluminium teapot and its knitted cosy, though I suspect that was my mother's idea.)

There was a lot of hate and escaping in my background and little continuity in places where ancestors have lived and died. It is a state of deracination leavened by research and scattered connections. How many people live like this? How many avoid rather than seek out family? How important is nationality and its determination by history, by birth, by mother tongue, by personal choice?

Innocent Reading for Origin is an artwork made by Elizabeth Gertzakis whose parents came to Australia from Greece in 1956 when she was two. The work is based on snapshot photos from her parents' lives. They are the sort of images often kept in a shoebox somewhere, in this case an Italian one under the bed, and brought out regularly in order to revive and share memories from other times and other places. The work consists of a series of very large black-and-white photographs. Though they were originally ordinary hand-sized photos from a family album, for exhibition they were enlarged as big as posters and each was flanked by an equally large block of text making a comment on it. The blocks of text voice a child's naïve commentary on the images. Their questioning tone exemplifies every child's ambivalence about the world that preceded their existence. This is the seeking of origin. The words are vivid and active. This is not the sanitised good family voice of respect, memory, recognition, genealogy and explanation but a rude voice of provocation and dissatisfaction, curiosity and even hostility. Thus it is shocking, private, and unexpected. As well as the child's innocence and misunderstanding it reveals some of the unsaid dimensions of family photos, the unspoken tensions and events underlying bodies and faces, clothes and demeanours. For example, next to an image of a woman dressed as a bride standing next to a man it says: 'Who is this lady I can't see? She is being dragged along. A cloth is pulling on her face. She looks full of mystery. She is all covered. I want to pull away the white to see her face, to see her eyes. It is all unclear. They are walking, she is being dragged.'

Gertzakis composes a new mythology from her family photos but it is not a neat handed-down and handed-on story; in fact there are no remembered family stories told here, rather a child's own jumbled and distorted version of events making unexpected connections and strange suggestions. It communicates the child's longing for information and sense. But somehow this personal story becomes exemplary of anyone's story, and also evidence that the way that stories or even accounts of historical events are told is often wilful or arbitrary. The artwork copes with awkwardness and strangeness, with disorientation and the unknown. It also – and this is its most telling point – uses ordinary everyday experiences as the subject for art, which is to say it reveals commonplace personal experience to be culture.

The work does not discuss place, migration or Greekness, it is simply presented as having happened, but clearly the photographs are tied to a particular time and place reminiscent of a post-war 1950s neo-realist aesthetic. The work tears open a corner of a container, an Italian shoebox, of stored feelings and memories, stored both against and for retrieval. And in this act it establishes an intimacy with the reader so that their interior voice too is felt as potentially shared or shareable. Translation and the movement of language across cultures distorts and fractures meaning. Yet it also leads to its potent multiplication.

Another artwork foregrounding language and translation is Simryn Gill's *Tree of Enlightenment* (1994) which combines leaves from the Bo tree (*Ficus religiosa*), famous for shading Gautama Buddha at the moment of his enlightenment, with dictionary definitions of words. Gill is a Malaysian Indian born in Singapore who spent her childhood in Malaysia and was educated in the UK and Australia. The work consists of seven glass bottles stoppered with corks and with cursive writing cut into their clear watery surfaces. Light catches in the engraved lines, white lines on transparent glass. They are the flat clear bottles used for spirits. The bottles sit on a long-legged metal table painted a dull grey. A skeleton Bo tree leaf has been rolled up and then released inside each bottle and lyrically occupies that space with its semi-invisibility. Going close to the bottles you look through the glass to the leaf which is filigreed and lacy, almost as if it has been written on, then you refocus your eyes to read the spidery writing incised into the surface of the glass. It isn't possible to focus on the leaf and the writing at the same time. The leaf is as long and as wide as the bottle. As you focus and refocus your eyes you sense the erotics of language, as the sensuality of the work, the unfurled leaves, the layerings and distortions draw your body in so that you look with your neck and back as much as with your eyes and mind.

The hand-engraved cursive writing is a series of definitions from a 'legendary dictionary of British India' of the apparently random words – Cheese, Muddle, Chop, Jack, Interloper, Solar and Sudden Death. Their complex and unexpected provenances reference Hindustani, Malay, Dutch, Tamil, Indian, Chinese, Bengali, English and pidgin English. They demonstrate the overlapping of cultures and the difficulty of tracing origins and even meanings in language. They encompass enormous passages of time and history, information and experience. The dictionary is clearly a colloquial one for a specific audience, and the implication may be that all dictionaries are equally regional.

The most unexpected definition is that for the word 'cheese'. On the glass is written:

CHEESE, 'Any thing good first rate, genuine, pleasant, or advantageous' (slng Dict.). The most probable source of the word is Hindi 'Chiz', 'thing'. For the expression used to be common eg: 'My new Arab is the real chiz'; 'These cheroots are the real chiz,' ie the real thing.

The historical and cultural events of colonisation loom large in the ripple effect of reading these definitions as they imply the journeys of people and habits, and words and power relationships, and transfers of knowledge and information. Worlds within worlds. One of them suggests the book was written by the Indians, not the English, as it refers irritably to the 'English people, led astray by the usual striving after meaning'. Gill's works hold both the tenuousness of meaning and the flexibility of language. Like items from a Tower of Babel they demonstrate the intertwinings of language that have come about throughout history and continue to affect what we say and what we think. The work holds out knowledge and enlightenment as illusory, but quite possibly beautiful. It shows that although you may expect a dictionary to lead you calmly through a linguistic trail it may be neither conclusive nor satisfying. But each time we learn another language, even just a few words, we expand our understanding of possible meanings and sounds waiting to be found.

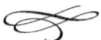

Today the dog and I walk in Chambers Gully. A short drive from our house off Waterfall Gully Road, it is an old quarry and dump site currently being replanted with indigenous vegetation. It is full of huge fig trees, towering fennel plants, and blackberries crowding the path of the creek that winds through. It is alive with bees working overhead, butterflies and birds swooping around, as well as small lizards and bugs darting about on the ground. The stillness of the air and the golden light slanting through from the west makes it seem as if we are in Paradise. As I stand still for a moment struggling with my genetic and environmental burden – Teutonic gloom and Celtic fatalism, Jewish chutzpah and an Irish tongue, mixed with the weight of American literal-mindedness and Australian irreverence, a butterfly comes to sit on my hand, not fresh but slightly tattered, its wings wave open and reveal bright blue eyes on each side. It lightly scratches my hand and stays there, giving me a small gift of presence and acceptance.

OCTOBER

reconstituting the ordinary

> ... it would be better for us that all the pictures in the world
> perished, than that the birds should cease to build nests.
> John Ruskin

There is something that I used to do regularly that I haven't done for a long time – lie down on my stomach on the ground outside and look at a tiny piece of earth in front of me, a place where nothing is happening. By staying still and watching, feeling the sun on my back, the wind in my hair, the sound of birds or bees, I usually find there is much activity happening on the ground. There are tiny blue flowers, and ants climbing the flower stems, slaters rushing through grass tunnels, yellow bugs drying their wings and launching off into first flights, cicadas vibrating with sound or crawling out of the earth, large brown stick-like grasshoppers disguised as twigs, millipedes making many-footed patterns as they flow along, seedpods splitting open and distributing their seed, ants collecting the seed plus a dead companion, and so on. The plants and the ground fill my view rather than being a block of colour somewhere below me. My next act is to roll over on my back, perhaps in a slightly different site where I am not quite so familiar with the teeming life beneath me and don't have to think too hard about bugs walking into my ears.

Then I make contact with the earth, feel its curve beneath my spine and see nothing but the sky above me. This double-sided encounter with the earth has the effect of creating a small zone of calm within me, of putting things into proportion, though it is not about rational thinking – rather the experience fills me with a sense of belonging and a kind of contentment. It is also a sensation of opening, and doing it as a child at the centre of the oval behind our house, a place fringed with large trees and roofed by a wide sky, is an experience fundamental to my ideas.

It is the sort of act that a child performs without reflection, opening to the world and finding it opening back. Becoming a parent and having to answer my own child's questions was a catalyst for me to think about issues of origin and belief. How far back can we, do we, go? How do we define origins and belonging? How do we learn about our ancestors? How do we define them or find them? Can we go on finding them all our lives? How do we decide what is important? To declare belonging may be one of the biggest declarations we make; it may happen inside a book, after a moment's acquaintance, or over thirty years.

Answering the big questions posed by children is an opportunity to know what we have made of what we have learnt through living, to find out what our position is while declaring it, but it can be a very complicated business. What we get, what we give, may not patch together into a cohesive universe. Nationality in particular can be like a basket of mixed fruit, including both insects and vipers. When people talk about the humourlessness of Germans it annoys me, as my father was quite good at telling jokes. He could be full of charm, though he was impossibly arrogant and rabidly paranoid, and when he was young, I have been told, was often 'deprassed'. He had a German accent which I never noticed till one day when he gave a talk at my school, and then all of a sudden in that context I heard it. Now he has gone, whenever I hear a German accent I feel great tenderness which arises somehow from my unknown affectionate feelings for this man who was so difficult to love. In general I like accents a lot as they make language sound new, they colour it and give it different shapes. I am even keen on misunderstandings in language as they also make life and thought richer. Often when I asked questions as a child my parents would reply, 'That's a very Jewish question' and not answer it. I learned a few Yiddish words like *kibbitz*, *kvetsch* and *mensch*. Both parents also always said that I must have kissed the Blarney Stone. My mother's father was Irish, purportedly a deserter from the Indian Army, sure a charmer. She on the other hand was pragmatic to the point of nihilism, something that always bugged me with my inexplicable shining store of hope and idealism, some of which I must surely have imbibed from attending primary school in America. I never recognised her approach to life as Celtic fatalism till hearing writer Alex Miller talk about his Irish mother and how once, when he told her the secret deep feelings that were in his heart, her only response was 'never mind, Al'.

All people are born with a sense of interconnectedness to the world. They may lose touch with it and then it has to be re-learnt or re-discovered or re-invented. Thinking that creation stories are important is not the same as creationism, the fundamentalist adherence to the Bible which is set against the teaching of evolution in schools in America. Actually evolution is a really good creation story packed full of wonder, and miracles. New creation stories might refer to how a person was made, how their point of view of the world was formed and how they are connected by history and knowledge, and by incidents and relationships, to other beings. A creation story might refer to how an artwork is made and to all the ideas and issues drawn into its fabric. An important aspect of contemporary Australian art is its vivid and urgent engagement with history and with nature. The opening of language and thought to correspondences and metaphors provided by nature connects all of us to everything else, putting us into perspective as creators, storytellers, namers, guardians, caretakers and custodians of the world.

I have often reflected on the words of anthropologist Peter Sutton about the potential influence of Aboriginal culture on Australian culture. He suggests that it would be valuable for Australians to re-imagine the suburb as the site of epiphanies and attachments:

It's possible that turning some of the intellectual lessons of Aboriginal art back onto how we understand the suburbia of the Fifties (60s, 70s, 80s, 90s) might help shift the balance towards something more firmly grounded in reality, for most Australians. It also might flesh out Australia's national self-representation with a little mainstream self-exoticism, reconstituting the ordinary as the powerful, as something we think we understand but seldom do without revisioning, without ritual.

Learning from Aboriginal culture does not mean all Australians embracing a whole series of Aboriginal beliefs and stories about the land, and taking over a spiritual landscape which is not theirs. It means paying attention to your locale, and understanding that everyday acts and events, even those which are not generally considered particularly cultural, are significant. Thus rather than seeing only big historical events as being 'real' history and 'real' culture, it means seeing history and culture as part of each individual and their life. As anthropologist Deborah Bird Rose points out, the sentiment of home is not dependent on perfection. 'Everywhere one goes in Aboriginal Australia, people describe their own homeland as "good country". From the bleakest sandhills to mosquito-infested swamps, each homeland is "good country" for the people who belong there.' Indigenous people bring to a wider society not only the richness of their diverse cultures and ways of organising and conceiving the world but above all a belief in and the practice of the importance of joining thought to feeling, to connect knowledge and emotion. This is becoming more and more relevant in our ecologically stretched times. All indigenous people regard the earth with great emotion as if it is sentient, a member of the family. So do many non-indigenous people.

Papua New Guinea artist Michael Mel has written about indigeneity as something open to all human beings. His description of it, through talking about his people, the Mogei, and their concept of *kanamb*, involves a notion of embodied knowledge meaning the dissolution of the binaries of observer and observed, individual and world. It means dropping divisions between objective and subjective, structure and meaning, inner and outer, material and spiritual, feelings and thoughts, culture and nature. In this way of thinking the self is experienced not as a container to be filled but as a series of relationships with all people living and dead, with people as individuals and with the physical world and all things around us. Any self is not separate but is engaged in and part of the world in an interconnected and interwoven whole. Making the intellectual and emotional leap to think about and maybe understand or feel this way of being and seeing contributes to an opening of the way we view the world and how we act in it.

Fiona Hall's art has been concerned for some time with ecology, with scientific taxonomy and with connections between all species. She says: 'We have discovered not only that we belong, as with all other living things, to a vast, genetically interrelated community but that we are direct descendants of the first replicator molecules.' Her artwork *Dead in the Water* is displayed inside a glass vitrine with a sheet of glass running horizontally through the middle of it, cutting the space in two as if the top half is air and the bottom half is water. It is an imaginary slice of the sea, lifted from that ever-moving vastness and placed in a typical museum case like a science diorama. Using small clear glass beads and silver wire Hall has recreated the forms of various marine creatures, spectacular transitional forms on the border of animal and vegetable life. They hang down in the water section of the case. Some of them have multiple openings, some of them have none; it is hard to tell whether they can see or which way is up. At the water level their bulbous extravagant bodies are joined to pieces of white plastic plumbing pipe that she has perforated into a dense sieve-like net of holes. The pipes sit above the glass like lacy periscopes.

This artwork expresses a complex hybridity as well as being a homage to the fertile and mutable ability of nature to incorporate and to encompass. The incapacity of the pipes to hold water contradicts their function. It suggests metaphoric leakages between life-forms, movements from culture to culture, gene to gene, the cross-infiltration of languages and thought. This permeability emphasises the interdependence and symbiosis of the world. Plastic plumbing pipe is very ordinary. In most places it has replaced metal pipes with its generic plain smooth whiteness and relative indestructibility. While metal corrodes and cement rots, plastic's longevity is unknown, ranging hypothetically from a hundred to a thousand years. The artwork's title *Dead in the Water* draws attention to the destructive work carried out at sea by plastic. More than a million seabirds and 100,000 mammals and sea turtles die globally each year from entanglement in, or ingestion of, plastics. On remote islands, inside tiny and large creatures, at the bottom of the sea and trailed along its many kilometres of beaches there are pieces of plastic. When you walk on the beach and sometimes think you have found a bright treasure, a rare shell or marine beast, often it will be a piece of plastic, its vivid colour and inert texture made almost lifelike by the weathering of the elements.

Current research into genetics also takes physical form in Hall's creatures in a vivid and complex manner. These are mythic creatures, linking plant and animal worlds, beings that, like those designed by Hieronymus Bosch, have missed the ark. They demonstrate the inspiration, exuberance and energy Hall finds in the folds and tufts, the fringes and lumps, squiggles, warts and knobs, the sheer inventiveness of the natural world. The artwork is about the teeming fertility of the creation of the world, its discovery and its destruction. The discoveries that Hall is concerned to draw attention to are those that show not only all people as equivalent to each other but equivalent to all other forms of life, not only animal but vegetable and even mineral: 'Now we know that the seemingly infinite, disparate variety of living matter on earth, of which we are but a part, is life's giant polymorphic skin, encasing us all, inside which we dwell in kindred, genetic proximity.'

The physical form of Hall's work, tiny beads threaded on fine wire and formed into intricate shapes, represents hours of time as well as her ingenuity and a correspondingly detailed intellectual heritage. Glass beads are participants in the history of colonialism, in the journeys of Empire. Glass beads, literally sand transformed by heat into a glittering precious substance, were used as trade items in attempts to influence native peoples. Impressive in their sparkling clarity and available in great quantities, they were used as precious treasure to be bestowed on people unaware of their actual negligible value. The intensity of Hall's work emphasises the importance of every dot, every cell, every breath of life on the earth. It draws attention to the past to emphasise its complexity and its close interrelationship with the present.

A series of woven rugs by Beth Hatton showing native Australian animals and titled *Endangered and Extinct Species* contain echoes for me of the *Powhatan Mantle*, an ancient Native American garment now housed at the Ashmolean Museum in Oxford. In recapitulating the emotional and practical aspects of recycling Hatton returns to memories of her childhood, growing up in rural Saskatchewan, Canada, where her grandmother and aunt made rag rugs from old clothes. Hatton uses kangaroo fur as well as sheep wool to make her rugs, thus bringing together the native animal with the introduced, the smudgy downiness of fur with the stout firmness of dyed wool, to tell their separate and interrelated stories. These works embody the issues that Hatton is concerned to explore, both haptically and intellectually. Each rug contains the fur of many kangaroos which she buys from a business associated with the pet food industry.

In some of Hatton's weavings a fingerprint and an animal's fur patterning are juxtaposed to emphasise human agency in the fate of the world, a power that can destroy or conserve. In other weavings the names of introduced animals are not woven but stencilled onto the red wool that imitates the colour of the iron-rich Australian soil. This stencilling, as a layer on top of the material rather than embedded in it, imitates the identification and classification markings on wool bales. The pastoral annals of Australia, an industry and history containing great emotional attachments and meanings for many people, are represented by these stencils in black ink of the simple words: cattle, sheep. The native animal names are actually woven into the rugs and thus visible from both sides of them – wallaby, bandicoot, wombat, dunnart, bettong, bilby – and they draw Aboriginal languages with them into the warp and weft of the fabric.

Of course all rugs were once pelts rather than objects manufactured by people; they were simply the skins of animals. Close connection to animals is part of having a fur rug, being with it and knowing it. In handling kangaroo fur Hatton has felt inklings of such knowledge. She writes: 'In past centuries human beings have coped with this spiritual dilemma by making some kind of covenant with the animals.' This would be a relationship incorporating a sense of responsibility towards their well-being, and compensatory and careful treatment of them as a resource for our well-being. The word 'covenant' suggests a sacred promise of immense proportions.

I first saw Hatton's work in a warehouse near Mildura where it was part of a large collection of artworks from more than one hundred artists gathered from all over Australia for the fourth *Mildura Palimpsest* exhibition in 2001. This exhibition of artworks, all concerned with the environment, was held in the vast decommissioned Aurora dried-fruit packing shed. Dividing walls the size of multi-storey buildings were built from hundreds of the large wooden crates in which the fruit was once collected. Being there was like walking into an Anselm Kiefer painting. Just before she hung it on the wall Hatton spread the Tasmanian Tiger rug over the bonnet of my old yellow station wagon. If she had turned her back it could easily have slipped inside the car to stay there as a car rug, to be used for picnics and naps. In fact I had a feeling that I knew that rug before I saw it. It would, of course, be a talking point at a picnic, bringing up questions about the environment and ecology, politics and science, wonder and joy. Should we eat kangaroo? Should the Tasmanian Tiger be cloned? How lovely it is to touch animal fur.

Another artwork that draws up forgotten or loose memories is *The Memory Line*, a temporary public artwork made by Jennifer Turpin and Michaelie Crawford in 1996. Though I didn't actually see it, a photograph and the concept of it remain in my mind with great tenacity. An event over time rather than an object, *The Memory Line* was made for *Restoring the Waters*, a project of the Australian Conservation Foundation in collaboration with the Fairfield City Council. The work took the simple form, in the medium of grass growing on grass, of the broad arabesque line made by an unfettered creek. In Western Sydney in Clear Paddock Creek in Fairfield, a 4-metre wide, 2.7-kilometre long swathe of rye-corn grass was planted on both sides of the banks of the channellised creek. When it reached one metre high it was mowed so that the grass marking the creek's original meandering course stood out softly and sinuously, looping next to and back and forth over the concrete stormwater canal to which it was confined in the seventies.

The temporariness of the artwork and of the grass correspond to the elusiveness of memory. When I return to a place from an earlier time in my life I get a tickling sensation somewhere in my body, maybe in my arm, leg, neck or back, a physical reaction as my body responds first, sensing the familiarity and memories that escape my mind. Similarly I feel the meanders, the eloquence, of *The Memory Line* in my body. The shape of water, the wide sweep made by a stream across flat land, has a currency deep in the human heart. All over urban areas in Australia marshes have been drained, creeks and streams forced underground, cemented over and turned into drains as an engineering response to water management. Today they are being uncovered and wetlands are being established for the health of the whole country. *The Memory Line* brought the memory of one creek back into vision and reintroduced the graceful curves of its path, drawing with grass on grass with immense delicacy like skin on skin, a hand caressing a back. It suggested that what has been destroyed or lost is still present and can be recalled and revived or renewed.

The *Restoring the Waters* project has since restored 550 metres of the creek to its original meanders. How many creeks are still under roads or inside drains holding the shape of earlier times and promising grace in an over-determined world?

Water and its meanderings as a synonym for memory appear in the writing of Toni Morrison who, in writing about the often apparently unrelated images floating around in her mind that she draws upon when writing a story, said: 'like water, I remember where I was before I was "straightened out".' She describes the Mississippi River and how it was straightened out in places to make room for houses. Occasionally the river floods back into these places. But it is not flooding, she writes, it is remembering. Remembering where it used to be. Writers are like that, according to Morrison, only they have emotional memory, the kinds of things remembered by the nerves and the skin. Her words connect with Turpin and Crawford's *Memory Line*. They suggest that we can go back to where we were before we were moulded to conform to certain needs or expectations of society. They imply a rhythm that is deep within us. They emphasise the significance of memory in drawing people back to their origins and to the important things they have to do. They also suggest that the stories which we do not hear at first or which are not on the surface might be the most important ones.

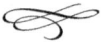

When we go out together I am very aware that the dog is never just walking but is always hunting, nose twitching, eyes darting around for anything that moves or has the density of a body. A dark clump of leaves can set him off, a hubcap or cardboard box by the side of the road can get him quite excited until he gets close enough to smell it. Sometimes I see it too and a crumpled newspaper takes on the dense form of a crouching cat before it dissolves back into paper.

At this time of year I forage for fruit when we walk, though all through the year I am looking for something to take home, a cutting of a geranium or a succulent, a distinctive stone or a quartz crystal, an aromatic piece of a cypress or something edible – mushrooms, blackberries, figs, olives, mulberries, peaches, lemons, lime leaves or grapes. October is the month of the loquats; pale orange and growing in clusters, they have slightly furry skin and large very shiny stones. The flesh is mostly sweet but can make you gasp if it is a bit sour. Sometime we visit specific trees while at other times we find trees laden with fruit by accident. Sometimes our regular trees have been removed but we always find others that we didn't know were there. I pick a bagful and eat them immediately. The loquats taste best if they are eaten while walking as they start to lose their firmness as soon as they are picked, and their skins and stones need to be removed – if you are walking you can spit them out as you go.

NOVEMBER

heart country

The silence on the floor of my house
Is all the questions and all the answers that have
been known in the world
Agnes Martin

Attached by a rusting drawing pin to the window frame that my desk faces is a large postcard showing the painting called *Six days in Nelson and Canterbury* by Colin McCahon. I love its hills, their volumes and quiet but insistent assertion of emotional space. The painting makes me think of a journey in a car. The six horizontal views included in it have the rough proportions of the front or rear windows of a car and are like those slices of land and sea and sky that you continually see moving past you as you drive along. Three views show mostly plains, while the other three show mostly hills, in rough sequences as if the car comes towards hills and then leaves them behind. They remind me of the moments in a familiar car trip where there is always some point at which you cross a rise or see something in the distance or take a particular turn and what you see becomes representative of the journey or of a particular part of that journey and the feelings associated with it – where the plain begins, where the mountains rise up or the bush starts, where you first glimpse the river, the sea, or the trees that mean the river is there, the shift in or beginning of a particular kind of vegetation like the mulga, the mallee, the smooth trees or the low trees, that bit of undulating road where you first see a landform rising in the distance and so on. They remind me of the way moods and feelings attach themselves to hills because of the way light folds on them, the way it starts, stops and caresses their masses and describes them, and the way light can show the flatness of a plain and the shadow at the edge of it. Thus the forms of landscape are touched within the body as well as with the eyes. Hills especially affect me, hills and mountains, in particular the country around Canberra, which I think of as my heart country.

In 1985 I was one of a few artists who painted murals on the outside of the artist-run Bitumen River Gallery in Canberra. I painted words written by Margaret Preston in 1927, important words on art as not about progress or a simple predictable path from beginner to expert: 'She does not imagine she has advanced in her art – only moved. The ladder of art lies flat, not vertical.' I painted it in homage to Preston and to the work of Colin McCahon whose work I saw at the 1984 *Biennale of Sydney* in a solo show called *I will need words*. McCahon's use of words was partly inspired by the text paintings of Uncle Frank, the evangelist relative of his friend and fellow painter Toss Woolaston, and the way he saw them used in fourteenth- and fifteenth-century Byzantine icons and in early Christian works such as Simone Martini's *Annunciation* painted in 1333. I was moved by the rawness and passion in McCahon's work, and especially by the *Elias* series of word paintings which deal with the moments just after Jesus said his last words: '*Eloi, Eloi, lama sabachthani?*' (My God, My God, why hast Thou forsaken Me?). It involves a mishearing, a misprint, a misunderstanding coming at a moment of incredible import, a moment when you feel nothing should be misunderstood.

AN OPENING

The story goes that many of the people standing beneath the cross misheard Jesus and thought he was talking about the prophet Elias who was lifted up to heaven by chariots and horses of fire and so they said 'Let be, will Elias come to save him?' and eagerly waited to see this spectacle. McCahon obviously likes this moment of confusion and outrageous voyeurism, of doubt and faith, and the phrase 'let be' for he repeats it. His ten *Elias* series paintings ask this question in various configurations of painted words: 'he calls for Elias let us see whether Elias will come to save him', 'will he save him let be let be will Elias come to save him? ever', 'was it worthwhile will could Elias save him save him', 'will he save him, let be let be'. They also answer the question with the words 'never', and 'why cannot can't he save him himself?', which is the question that has always struck me as the most memorable. It is one of those phrases that comes back to haunt me, being partly about self-reliance and partly about being in a hopeless position. Drawing attention to the story of such an important religious moment being full of misunderstanding and misinterpretation shows the prevalence of them in our lives, even or especially at important moments. Why can't we save ourselves? Maybe we can.

The *Elias* paintings are made on hardboard using ordinary enamel house paint with added sand and sawdust for texture. They are very powerful in their simplicity and the sense of enormous recessive spaces of sky and land opening up behind the words. They are the sort of spaces that you might see through your fingers after a night of tears as the windows start to lighten with the dawn, or that you might see in the landscape at dusk with rain or mist blurring shapes, shifting distance and making monumental what is ordinary. The sense of a voice in the paintings through the necessity of reading the words and thus hearing that voice in your head, hectoring and querulous, sometimes booming, full of both faith and doubt, religious but not only religious, also everyday, and, embedded in the painting behind the painted words, the layers of colour like emotions, involving soft fades and transitions from dark to light like morning or evening skies though in ochre reds and yellows, all these things are insistently present in the works. As well as, of course, silence.

The work in my postcard *Six days in Nelson and Canterbury* was painted by McCahon in 1950 from his memories of riding a bicycle looking for seasonal work in the regions of Nelson and Canterbury in New Zealand. But rather than suggesting any careful transcription of specific places or long hours bent over preparatory drawings it contains essential elements only, and the six views are like dream landscapes, felt places, in which detail has given way to shadows and heavy silences. They contain the deep longing and contemplation evident within the look of mountains and plains when the light is fading or forming and everything becomes simplified. The six views are separated by thick black lines which do not frame or outline the works but branch out unevenly from a central vertical black line. Within the central line is a long narrow V of red paint almost invisible in the black. McCahon said that the red represents the blood of Christ, as well as his own that he shed when he had a fall from his bicycle. McCahon's son William has said that this work was influenced by Leonardo da Vinci's painting *The Virgin of the Rocks*. When you look at reproductions of the two paintings together you can see that what McCahon has borrowed is the sense of deep space, an almost infinite depth, achieved by da Vinci's placement of distant landscapes of rocks on either side of the Virgin, landscapes which recede deeply into the background by virtue of both their scale and the illuminated sky behind them which appears to be immensely far away. The light-filled skies in both da Vinci's and McCahon's landscapes punch holes into the paintings, places for our eyes to travel deeply, and our thoughts to expand into limitlessness.

The title *Six days in Nelson and Canterbury* refers to a journey by the artist and also to the six days of creation described in the Bible. McCahon is imagining God creating not only the entire world, but also New Zealand, a place virtually undepicted and unknown in European art. If God created the world then he also created New Zealand. God's Own Country, often abbreviated to Godzone, is a phrase that has been used for more than 120 years by New Zealanders to describe their homeland. The earliest recorded use of the phrase was as the title of a poem about New Zealand written in the 1880s. Lots of countries, maybe all of them, think of themselves as God's own country, but being so far away from most other countries New Zealand is especially sensitive about it. In the central painting of another work by McCahon called *Northland triptych*, above a cloud like a pink bruise hanging over a yellow hill with a crack in it, McCahon writes in black paint 'New Zealand why does nobody love you' referring to the short European history of New Zealand and thus the absence of a place for New Zealand in English-speaking culture. He is also thinking about the drastic environmental devastation practised upon the land by its European inhabitants.

New Zealand was one of the last habitable land masses in the world to be settled. Migrants sailed in double-hulled canoes from East Polynesia. Many methods have been used to determine the date when they first arrived. Although no single method is foolproof, all agree that permanent Polynesian settlement was established around 1300. Maori genealogies (*whakapapa*) include the names of the canoes in which they first arrived in New Zealand, thus though they are considered indigenous people and have creation stories for New Zealand, their arrival is part of their story. Yet the Maori call themselves *tangata whenua*, the people of the land.

How flexible is the idea of indigeneity? How is connection to place made and maintained? When I was a child indigenous peoples were invisible and talked about as if they were extinct and legendary like the dodo. Today it is impossible not to know that many if not all indigenous peoples have survived into the twenty-first century. In Australia there is a turning point at which you suddenly really see or feel the land for the first time as Aboriginal land. Such encounters are different for each person. It may happen by seeing a movie or a TV show, hearing something on the radio or reading a book about powerful feelings for country, about dispossession, about language and family groups. Or it may be an exhibition of some art that speaks and opens a door. Or you hear someone speak, or dance or sing. Or you are shown a carved tree or artefacts which previously you would have seen as pieces of stone and suddenly realise that artefacts are all around you. At this point you are enabled to see that much of Australia once held voices and movements very different from what it does now, and that it wasn't that long ago. This is a point at which you see the past as still present, still living, still part of the future. Each person can trace their own understanding of this revelation. Once your eyes are opened it's everywhere. And you see indigeneity not as something belonging to the past or a stage in the evolution of human development that has been superseded but as miraculously present. A couple of times I went on a tour of rock art sites in the Adelaide Hills and saw paintings and engravings as well as tiny pieces of stone that had been tools. Since then I see each fragment of rock as a potential artefact. Walking or driving around Adelaide you often see trees with shelters in their bases or that have had oval-shaped pieces of bark of various sizes removed from them.

Babakiueria, a short film directed by Don Featherstone in 1986, introduces an Australia in reverse. It shows a country occupied by white Australians who are having a barbecue when a boat of Aboriginal people arrives on the shore. 'What is this place called?' ask the Aboriginal people. 'It's a barbecue area', the white people reply. We then see Aboriginal people as policemen dealing with errant white people whose children need to be taken away from them and who lose their home and most of their rights at the same time. This role reversal is humorous and cutting. Some of the white people protest this treatment while others are compliant and go quietly. The black journalist narrator tells us that she has always been interested in white people, and though we hear this statement all the time about Aboriginal culture or Aboriginal people it is seen to be both intrusive and odd when a simple colour change is made. Seeing this film late one night by accident on TV in my lounge room in Canberra was a highly entertaining shock.

Another work on black/white relationships that I can't forget is Joy Hardman's video *I Spy* (1997). She went to live in Alice Springs in 1995 and made a work about what she found there. It is unusual in its frankness, which is partly explained by the fact that she had only been there for two years. It played on a TV installed on a bit of sand in the front gallery at the Contemporary Art Centre of South Australia. It is most confronting in its honesty, showing her talking, well whispering actually, and you need to listen a few times to hear it all, about the complexities of the relationships between blackfellas and whitefellas in Central Australia. Her words do not talk up either the integrity of the blacks or of the whites but tell something of the ongoing strange workings between the two. For many reasons such things are often left unspoken.

In the video Joy, a white woman, wearing khaki shorts and

shirt and boots sits cross-legged on the ground holding alternately small pieces of mica, little leaves, crushed drink cans and tiny feathers over her eyes and whispering to the video camera:

I spy with my little eye something that starts with W, I spy whitefellas trying to help blackfellas, I spy ... whitefellas and blackfellas drinking a lot of alcohol, I spy ... whitefellas going to work and blackfellas going to social security, I spy ... whitefellas making gender politics out of blackfella business, I spy ... whitefellas spying blackfellas as the real people at peace with the universe, as more spiritual, as holding answers to bad whitefella ways.

Riddle riddle me ree there's something I can see and it starts with B ... I see blackfellas with arms and legs in bandages, I spy ... blackfellas watching Jacky Chan videos and eating McDonald's in the MacDonnell Ranges, I spy ... whitefellas and blackfellas being careful about what they say about money and blackfella politics.

At this stage the camera pulls back and we see she is sitting cross-legged on the ground with a series of objects placed in front of her – a glass bowl of water, a shiny metal teapot, a rock, a glass sphere and finally a long piece of mirror. She handles each object and makes 'magic' gestures over them while whispering:

I see ... blackfellas with tins on strings like horses with hay bags around their necks, I see ... whitefellas writing and filing reports on blackfellas and blackfellas talking in local language about odd whitefellas ways; I see ... whitefellas believing they've been specially selected to learn blackfella secrets ...

and the video loop begins again.

'Missionaries, misfits and mercenaries' is the cynical phrase used to describe those who work with remote indigenous communities in Australia, but Hardman replaces the 'misfits' with 'mystics' in the statement that goes with her work. Her video responds eloquently to her experience of daily confrontations on the border between cultures in an unsentimental oscillation between reality and unreality, romanticism, comedy and tragedy.

Anne Mosey originally travelled to Central Australia in 1989 to retrace the footsteps of her great-great-grandfather, the explorer Peter Egerton-Warburton. Mosey discovered another country lying within the Australia she knew, a country of prior ownership and belonging whose stories both incorporated and exceeded those concerning her family. As soon as she arrived Mosey began to meet people and to engage with them. When she finally made her trip retracing the steps of her great-great-grandfather she was travelling with seventeen Warlpiri and Pintupi traditional owners. Thus she learned at firsthand of the mingled relationships and obligations of white/black relationships and the impossibility of simply moving through the country as if it was empty before European explorers entered it.

Some of the works Mosey made about Central Australia were collaborations with Dolly Nampitjinpa, now deceased. The first time they had a conventional exhibition, Dolly showed paintings, while Anne showed drawing and photographs, in a show about cross-cultural collaboration called *Commitments* at the Institute of Modern Art in Brisbane in 1990. After that they were invited by curator Tony Bond to do an experimental installation for the *9th Biennale of Sydney* in 1992. Dolly came up with the idea of showing her living space and Anne decided to complement it with hers. This first re-creation of their respective living quarters was called simply *Untitled*. They re-staged it at the University of South Australia Art Museum in 1994 and called it *ngurra (camp/home/country)*, (*ngurra* is a Pitjanjatjara word that means camp and home and country). The installation placed Anne Mosey's kitchen in Alice Springs and Dolly Nampijinpa's humpy at Yuendumu side by side like a traditional museum display of habitats.

The Art Museum, now demolished, was a large white cube

with a parquet floor and a vaguely disintegrating ceiling. Mosey set up her kitchen in a corner of it. It looked like a stage-set or a replica of a low rent holiday cabin, only crowded with too much furniture – cheap wood-veneer cupboards, two armchairs and a formica-covered table with two metal and vinyl chairs. There was a TV playing on a tea-chest, a gas stove, a fridge, a washing machine. Some books, a few Aboriginal dot paintings and several photographs made one wall more personal. Many people would feel like they knew this place already, half-office, half-home – ordinary transient accommodation. It was a fairly harsh room that could be imagined as cold and bleak in the morning or, lit with a fluorescent tube or two, steamy with the cooking of food in the evening, or warmed with conversation and endless cups of tea. Depending on our experience it could be imagined as the scene of recriminations and account-keeping of either the emotional or financial kind, a typical white person's quarters in a remote area work situation.

Next to this kitchen was a rough shelter made from about six sheets of corrugated iron, a large tarpaulin and some stout sticks. An upright forked piece of wood holding up the roof pole of the shelter was stuck in a large tin of red sand. Other strong sticks leant against the shelter. Apparently multipurpose tools, they were not just pieces of wood but recognisably parts of trees, retaining the lines of growth and the bark that characterised their species. A hearth consisting of a sheet of corrugated iron on which four blackened tin cans held up a grate lay on the ground. Inside the shelter there was a pile of blankets and tarpaulins lying alongside a cardboard box with supplies in it. Rubbish lay around, and there were some big drums with '16 KG Flour, Eudunda, SA, packed for The NT' written on them. There was a coolamon full of seeds and some spinifex. The roof pole of the shelter faced east/west. It was easy to imagine this shelter not in a gallery but on the ground under the stars as a nomadic dwelling, an Aboriginal camp site, easily able to be moved when a new location was required.

The general impression of both Anne and Dolly's camps was of shocking harshness and minimalism. The indigenous side of the equation was the most minimal and contained many objects clearly used for multiple tasks, like those stout sticks. The accompanying catalogue included interviews with each artist by anthropologist Petronella Vaarzon-Morel. Dolly's words, a short extract of which appears below, were printed in the catalogue in Warlpiri as well as translated into English.

This place we have is our home. In it we have our swags, blankets and billycans for tea. We also cook meat in it on the ground. A White person's house is different. He's got good cupboards, a phone to listen to and to talk with someone who is faraway. We have nothing. We just live in humpies. We only get our news from a person who has come from faraway. White people have everything different. They have very good houses and they are clean. Aborigines' homes are untidy. The billy cans are dirty, and dogs lick tea and soup from the billycans. A White person has a clean house, clean cupboards and rooms and he's got a bed, table and a very good kitchen which he uses in a lot of different ways.

We Aborigines have nothing. We have a few things like branches, blankets and a small swag. A White person has plenty of things, everything. White people only know about reading papers to get news from faraway places. They have a lot of books and papers for themselves. They don't have Dreamings. They haven't got them, nothing. Aborigines have sacred things. In that way they are rich. They know their Dreamings. Now, today, though they've got paper, and they know about liquor. Well Aborigines got that from the White people.

Anne's words, some of which appear below, were not translated into Warlpiri.

From an emotional and philosophical perspective the commonalities between us are the reason for doing the work — not the final aesthetic or the final product. The fact that we've worked together, that she was the chairwoman for the Women's Centre and I was the co-coordinator, the fact that we've travelled together, that she's taught me dancing and singing, that I've taken her and other women on yawulyu journeys, and that we've worked on the night patrol and so on. For me the connections are much stronger than the differences. But of course, what is seen are the differences, not the connections because they are invisible.

Connections can be made in many ways. A series of ten photo-compositions called *Patterns of Connection* (1992) by Leah King-Smith layer and superimpose historical archival images of Aboriginal people from the Picture Collection of the State Library of Victoria with landscape imagery hand-coloured with paint. The work merges the layers seamlessly so that, as is King-Smith's stated aim, we see these indigenous people 'in a positive and spiritual light'.

To describe a few of them is to try to put into words the amalgam of images they involve and their effect. A circular edge of darkness at the top of each photograph makes the viewer feel as if they are looking into a camera lens or a mirror. A white-haired Aboriginal man dressed in European clothes holds a boomerang and poses for the camera. Behind him a couple of white houses can be seen. A white dog with its back to the camera watches him. Up in the sky the arc of the edge of a river appears, trees are reflected in its water. In another image four Aboriginal women wearing white dresses sit in a row. Again, looking at the photograph is like looking through a portal into another time zone and a layer of clouds and trees and reflections is both within, over and above them. It is as if they are spirit beings behind glass in another world, the past, though perhaps it is we the viewers who are behind glass. In yet another image an old Aboriginal man, who looks like a poet or a prophet with a big cloak pinned over his shoulders, looks out of the centre of a photograph, layered inside him is a lake reflecting the sky and a large tree that is lined up with his backbone.

An intense sense that the people are in the land and that the land is in the people is conveyed by these images, but this is an inadequate description; rather the land is the people, the people are the land, they are one. The works were made in response to a commission to produce a book using some of the photographs of surviving Aboriginal people taken in the nineteenth century at the missions of Coranderrk, Ramahyuck and Lake Tyers, from the collection of the State Library of Victoria. Unexpectedly, the artist transformed the stereotypical view of them as bereft people decimated by loss and betrayal into images of people who are found and whole, strong and almost eternal. Notions of resilience, deep time and connectedness with nature are strikingly present in the works. King-Smith's hope is that the work will 'trigger people's inner perceptions rather than their outer kind of objective, pragmatic mode of understanding'. When first exhibited in Melbourne the works were shown with an environmental soundscape by Duncan King-Smith based on recordings made in the Victorian bush. In his words, it sought to 'open up the channels for communications from the spiritual force that nurtures natural places'.

Three artworks, made by Bea Maddock, between 1987 and 1998, display her growing understanding of the Aboriginal occupation of Australia combined with an attempt at understanding her own position in the same country. Each work repeats images of land and uses language in order to emphasise the importance of naming in claiming place and in asserting connection. In *we live in the meanings we are able to discern* an explorer's settlement and a vaguely arctic-looking coastline are carefully outlined and coloured-in like a children's book illustration. We see a small encampment with an Australian flag and a snowy outcrop of mountain, its head hidden in cloud. It is Heard Island, said by archaeologist Rhys Jones to be what Tasmania was like in the last Ice Age. Three lines of script run along the bottom of the seven-panelled drawing – they are Tasmanian place names in an Aboriginal language: *minnerronene winnibberler manwoneer* .... *mubberlee towwenric*. The simple charcoal drawing is filled in with encaustic – a painting technique in which wax rather than oil or water is used to hold pigment. It is a slow way of working because the wax, which needs to be kept molten, soon hardens, so brush strokes have to be very small. The work gains a degree of luminosity but also a sense of remoteness from the viewer with this technique. Below the drawings are small boxes. In each one there is an identical blurred blue-tinged photograph of the scene in the drawing. All at once map, drawing, photograph, object, the work is both neat and handmade in its construction. It also has a bit of a backyard feel to it. Its title *we live in the meanings we are able to discern* is an offering of great thoughtfulness suggesting as it does a potent mixture of limitation and possibility. If we don't know a lot we won't be able to understand very much, but as our knowledge expands we will have more meanings to live in. Yet 'discern' is such a subtle word; it suggests intuition and feeling as much as information and knowledge. Thus the artist proffers the significance of attentiveness to what may not be taught or said aloud but is nevertheless present.

Another work by Maddock, *Tromanner forgive us our trespass*, is a series of dry pale drawings, again made with the slow movements of encaustic, this time showing a bleached-out view of rolling yellow hills in Tasmania stretched over by a pale blue sky holding a few white clouds. There are five panels and on their lower edge are written cursive words in a Tasmanian Aboriginal language:

miemtina poimina poymatang ... their soft rhythms echo the soft cadences of Aboriginal voices. This time there are Aboriginal artefacts collected by the artist, wrapped and tied with string, in the small shelves beneath the images. Tromanner could be a misspelling or mishearing of Truganini, a name well-known as that of the purported last Tasmanian Aboriginal woman. And maybe the title of the work is a clue that the words beneath the drawing are a translation of *The Lord's Prayer*. As Christianity and the writing down of indigenous languages often go hand in hand, prayers are often the first things to be translated and written down. Here the land appears to have been cleared and exposed, bare tree trunks are visible across the painting. To think of it in relation to forgiveness and trespass makes it seem especially bleak and filled with loss. The waxy images are unevenly covered with white lines as if they have been clawed or scratched. It could be the white lines of rain but the land looks so dry. When you read the text or say it to yourself it is like a chant.

In Maddock's last work to be discussed here, *TERRA SPIRITUS ... with a darker shade of pale,* she incised the entire coastline of the island of Tasmania, viewed as if approached from the sea, onto paper, which was then rubbed with red ochre. Neither a drawing nor a print, the mark we see is a line embossed into paper with a dentist's steel probe, a line which would be invisible but for the colouring rubbed over it. The artist was going to make the drawings from a boat in the water but when she found out how impractical an idea that was she learnt how to use graph paper and maps to translate the coast into lines on paper. In a talk she gave on the way the work was made she told of collecting ochre locally around Launceston, of grinding it and mixing it with gum tragacanth, a traditional binder used in artist materials sometimes also called gum dragon, to make her own drawing pastels. She also made a bookbinder's tool from a bone she took from a dead dog that she found on the road. She used the tool to polish the surface of the paper depicting the sea. This was important because she had read that the Aboriginal people believed that when they died their spirits went into the sea.

Beneath the coastline the names of places in Tasmanian Aboriginal languages appear in neat cursive script in a paler shade of ochre; beneath them in blind (un-inked) typesetting are European place names. This detailed work of fifty-one images is a massive undertaking, a labour of love. At the same time it is awkward and has something of the quality of a primer, a first attempt at something, in this case reflecting on co-ownership and joint naming rights. But there is a disparity here in that while the European names are clearly documented the Aboriginal place names are less numerous and less precisely known. The drawing is reminiscent of the coastline images drawn by explorers and cartographers, archetypal first views, full of the promise and unfulfilled dreams of a mirage, of landfall, of first recordings of first sightings, even though the land was already known by those who lived there. *TERRA SPIRITUS* is a slow and measured view of the land that seems to contain none of the intense emotion and memory of Colin McCahon's *Six days in Nelson and Canterbury*, but its text layers create the sense of a soft murmuring, a slurring susurration of sound, something like that made by the sea when running onto the shore.

Colin McCahon often used words in his paintings, sometimes English, sometimes Maori. Frequently painted in black and white, McCahon's words speak, but also just are. They exist as objects as much as they are words. Thus language becomes as solid as paint, as palpable as skin. The light behind McCahon's words or the light coming through them puts them in vast geographic spaces set against the sky, and gives them a tremendous sense of movement and power. The eloquence, the potential wideness, of the words, of speech, becomes visible.

In the painting *The Lark's Song (a poem by Matire Kereama)* that he made in black and white acrylic paint on hinged doors, McCahon transcribed words from the book *The Tail of the Fish: Maori Memories of the Far North*. According to Matire Kereama, an elder of the Aupori tribe who wrote the words down from memory, *The Lark's Song* is the transcription of a popular children's song – a rhyme, a challenge, a kind of charm that must be said in as few breaths as possible. She said that to imagine it you must think of being a child lying on the grass with other children and making up words for the songs of the birds flying and singing above you. Poet and critic Wystan Curnow puts it thus:

> *McCahon wants us to defer translation so that we see the language as opaque, not transparent, so that we are held suspended among voices of children, saints, poets and painters – in language as such, where origin and impulse, natural and cultural, Maori and European, are all to be apprehended, but only as being in translation.*

This understanding of translation casts it as movement, process, an act of metamorphosis and transformation, an experience involving the body as well as the mind, and a generator of new ideas. At the very bottom of the painting McCahon quotes some words from a poem by Peter Hooper to invoke another person who talked to birds. He asks: 'Can you hear me St Francis?'

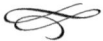

Because the paths from home are so well-worn we often get in the car and drive somewhere else for our morning walk. Sometimes we walk near where painter Dorrit Black lived, and pass the corner where she had her fatal accident. Often we go to a park near an oval where cricketer Donald Bradman once hit 330 runs in an afternoon and where Aboriginal people were last recorded as dancing in 1910. If we go to the foothills we walk on part of the Pioneer Women's Trail where German girls and women walked all night, probably singing hymns, from Hahndorf carrying eggs and vegetables to sell at the Adelaide markets. At the creek at the base of the hill they are said to have washed their feet and put their shoes on. We climb the hill and the higher we get the more I can see of the white dunes on the other side of the gulf like mirages in the distance.

We often flush out flocks of birds hiding in the grass which only take to the air when we are almost upon them. Pink-chested galahs, magpies, sulphur-crested cockatoos, wrinkle-eyed corellas, all like to sit on the ground and ferociously dig into the soil with their beaks. When crested pigeons fly they make a creaky noise as if their wings are squeaking.

Tonight we walk after many hot days under a cool sky, at last, while pink, grey and white elephant, whale, lizard and rat shaped clouds slide over our heads. Sometimes I sing, sometimes we see people standing in the dark smoking, watering the garden or staring up at the sky. Occasionally I speak to someone and bring home stories, like the one about the house where a very frail old lady lives by herself, and when we look into her house before she closes the venetian blinds the dining room is formally set with silver candlesticks and decanters on the sideboard. Another woman was wiring together two panels of her corrugated-iron fence and told us that it didn't need to last long as it wouldn't be long before she was gone, that is to say dead. Then there was the man with his rake stuck up a tree bringing down the last leaves, too impatient to let them fall. And a house where a man was painting a paling fence and a small boy kept saying excuse me, excuse me and I didn't realise he was trying to get my attention until he asked me, eventually shouting down the street: 'What is the name of your dog?' This is the question that all children ask.

DECEMBER
The drawing of correspondences

*They say in Asia it is not a miracle to walk on water
but on the earth.*
Trinh T. Minh-ha

There's a woodcut print of a dingo with a cheeky grin on my mantelpiece. I made it at the end of my first year of art school in 1982. It is black and reddish brown on off-white Japanese paper, an image of graphic vividness and energy. It is based on my drawing of a wooden dingo made at Aurukun in 1962.

When I visited the Institute of Anatomy in Canberra with my first year art school class we went there to do some drawing. The Institute was a short walk from the art school. Drawing was a large part of the curriculum; students in every workshop did hours, days, months and years of life drawing and general drawing, and printmaking students like me did even more drawing. At twenty-seven I was untrained in drawing and had the impossible dream of staying that way. I had a clear sense of the virtue of being raw, of using very basic materials, never using an eraser but turning mistakes into sense and being completely engaged, sincere, direct and never ever mannered. Each day our drawing lecturers would come up with a project for us to do, a different approach to drawing or different materials to see what we might do with them. A lot of the time I was both embarrassed and elated, not 'good' at art like most of the people around me but at last fulfilling my dream of being at art school, not wanting to be told what to do or how to do it, but to be initiated nonetheless.

For the excursion to the Institute of Anatomy I remember that rather than buying a drawing pad I prepared my own paper for the class. I bought large sheets of cartridge paper from the school shop and tore them, rather roughly, into rectangles that were about the size of an old half-carved woodblock plate I found in the art school bin to use as a drawing board. I attached the stack of paper to the board with crocodile clips. I drew with a thick French 2B graphite stick, a wonderful soft silvery six-sided block of 'lead', like a pencil, only as thick as my forefinger and with no wooden casing, so it made my hands grey and gave them a faint scent of metal.

First we went to the Anatomy Gallery of the Institute where human and animal skeletons, babies and body parts in bottles strongly smelling of formaldehyde were lined up in cases, as well as articulated animal skeletons posed naturalistically on branches. In the Ethnographic Gallery on the other side of the courtyard were Aboriginal artefacts from all over Australia, and in a series of glass cases the very special sculptural works made by the Wik people and collected at Aurukun on Cape York by anthropologist Frederick McCarthy in 1962 on a trip he made especially to get them and to record the ceremonies that went with them on film and in photos.

A row of wooden catfish hung down from a structure as if they were being dried, a fat mullet was laid down like a club, a shark bared its teeth, several dingoes smiled, a plover stood with its wings outstretched, the elder and younger Apalach brothers stood side by side – the shorter one covered in white dots, the taller with spikes sticking out of his arms. There was also an echidna and a wallaby, and the crippled boy of Thaa'puunt. I drew them all with my graphite stick. I remembered the displays in the ANU archaeology department of ancient Greek golden earrings, fragments of delicate iridescent glass, and red and black ceramic shards from old Egyptian pots, and how they seemed to hold the past. I studied the forceful eloquent forms of the Wik sculptures and the way that they were put together with simple wooden plugs and mortice and tenon joints. They were painted red, black, white and soft ochre browns with gritty earth pigments, and they had teeth made from sharpened bones and eyes carved from wood or made from glass beads, buttons, seeds or shells. They were not mannered or slick but sincere and direct, made carefully but with energy and a direct informality, and without over-controlled or over-finished surfaces. I remembered the energy and vitality of animals in books I knew from those drawn by Hugo Lofting for *Dr Dolittle*, the Moomintrolls and other beings drawn by Tove Jansson for her books, John Tenniel's illustrations for Lewis Carroll's *Alice in Wonderland*, E.H. Shepard's illustrations for *Winnie the Pooh* and *The Wind in the Willows*, May Gibbs's images for *Scotty in Gumnut Land*, as well as underground comics featuring Zippy the pinhead, the Furry Freak Brothers and Mr Natural, all drawings showing how the angle of a mere line or dot can change the expression of a face and thus an entire story. All the stories of mythological beings and metamorphosis in a series of books at the local library of myths, legends and folk tales from around the world that I used to read repeatedly as a child many years before, also came together, and I drew.

Unschooled and unskilled I drew, crudely with trepidation and doubt, but with affection and attention straight from the heart. I especially remembered my dog Maud who had died the year before. Maud was a Staffordshire terrier whom I first met when she belonged to someone else and I thought she was the ugliest dog I had ever seen. We became very close and when her owners moved I became her new owner. Our friendship, based on walking, talking, being together and feeling loved, was very powerful and deep. In the concentration of drawing everything came together – observation, memory, feelings.

The next week back at the printmaking department, visiting Japanese woodcut artist Akira Kurosaki started to teach us the traditional way to make Japanese woodblock prints. First he instructed us to transfer a drawing to very fine transparent Japanese paper by doing a brush drawing in black ink over a pencil drawing, then when it was dry pasting that brush drawing face down onto a piece of wood and carefully cutting out with a knife and a chisel whatever was not black. Then we learned to print from the woodblock onto thin Japanese paper. First this involved registering the paper with lines cut into a separate L-shaped piece of wood which sat against one corner of the block so as to be able to centre the paper on the block and be able to replace it in that position for subsequent application of colours or another layer of ink. The black Japanese ink mixed with a watery rice glue was brushed onto the block with a wide brush. If you wanted grey you added more glue, or even water for a broken texture. After the paper was laid on top of the block a rubbing tool or traditional baren made from circles of cardboard and a coil of tightly wound string covered with a mottled bamboo leaf was rubbed hard on the back of the paper to transfer the ink to the paper. Each layer of ink had to be printed twice. 'Nice image', said Kurosaki.

Many people thought my dingo print was a comment on Azaria Chamberlain who was taken by a dingo at Yulara in 1980, though that had never occurred to me, but I knew there was a lot of Maud the Staffordshire terrier, her huge smile and sturdy body in it. And the ferocity inside her gentleness. Working in the printmaking workshop at the same time was Banduk Marika from Yirrkala making linocuts, and from north-central Arnhem Land brothers-in-law Johnny Bulun Bulun and Jack Wunuwun making their first lithographs. Several of the people who were staff or students at the Canberra School of Art at the time, such as Theo Tremblay, Basil Hall and Martin King, have famously gone on to work as master printmakers with countless indigenous artists all over Australia. Some fellow students questioned whether my print made from my drawing of the Aurukun dingo was appropriating Aboriginal culture so I asked Banduk what she thought. She recognised the dingo from its markings as coming from Cape York, but said that she thought that if you did not just copy something but made it your own it was OK, and that I had made it my own.

It is ironic that with my aversion to judgements and strict categories in art I began in 1988 to work as a freelance art critic. Not always happy in this role, I can certainly say that it has been a passionate one. One way or another I rarely write in a disengaged manner; I always seem to care too much and regularly feel horror and nausea as well as joy and pleasure, while trying always to remind myself that the business of art involves other factors beyond my emotions. Nevertheless I am stuck with them. At least I have learned not to say when an artist's work makes me feel like throwing up. To each exhibition I try to bring a fresh eye to write about it for people who may never see it. I try to understand, to empathise in order to be able to convey the material and intellectual experience of the work. I imagine a person sitting at a table reading it, maybe somewhere remote, who will never see the art, having it brought to life in their minds by my writing and then taking it into their life as an experience that they may even tell other people about.

In pursuing my own artwork I swing widely between seeing what I am doing clearly and not knowing, between making work with fluency and sureness and having no idea what to do. I look earnestly in myself for just a little of the single-minded fortitude that I read in the eyes and the body of our dog every day, or the bird that sits cleaning its feathers outside my window. One thing I want is to find a way of communicating an identification with animals and plants and the non-human world, a vision of oneness or communion. Sitting very still and smoking a cigarette and then just breathing and hearing music in the wind is one way I used to merge with the world, but I rarely smoke these days.

I am talking about connection, about something that belongs to the earth and her inhabitants that is not the province of any one culture, something that Claude Lévi-Strauss described so well in *Triste Tropiques:*

During the brief interval in which our species can bring itself to interrupt its hive-like activity, [let us grasp] the essence of what it was and continues to be, below the threshold of thought and over and above society; in the contemplation of a mineral more beautiful than all our creations; in the scent that can be smelt at the heart of a lily and is more imbued with learning than all our books; or in the brief glance, heavy with patience, serenity and mutual forgiveness, that, through some involuntary understanding, one can sometimes exchange with a cat.

Or a dog.

Through exhibitions, books, articles and catalogues Aboriginal art joins the art of other places in history, galleries, institutions and syllabuses, but it would be tragic if the new things, the different things, the fresh and important things that it has to teach us are lost in this incorporation. It is a located art that asserts emotional relationship to place at the same time as, in the most impressive works, engaging with interlocked graphic, aesthetic and conceptual concerns such as opacity and transparency, layering and juxtaposition. These are not merely formal concerns attached to any one culture or period of art in the world, they are features of human image-making in a world in which when paint dries, like water retreating from the edge of a lake, it leaves a certain pattern. They register on our senses and connect with our emotions sublingually, beneath language, as well as being metaphors for thought.

Aside from all its specific cultural connections Aboriginal art demonstrates that art begins from and returns to human experience in the natural world and engages with the task of integrating human experience within it in a social, personal and historical way. Aboriginal art does not speak to us from another world but from another culture responding to this world. The ability of a medium such as paint to speak, not only English, not only Warlpiri, not only Pintupi, French, German or Italian, but a series of graphic tongues with their origins in parts of the world around us such as the clouds, the lines on our hands and the rhythms of the earth we all see and know, are what make it possible for the art of a nomadic people who have been living on this land for thousands of years to be able to communicate with sedentary people who arrived recently bringing with them the habits and preconceptions of other places.

An artist who painted at Warmun (Turkey Creek) in the Kimberley in Western Australia, Rover Thomas, made artwork with the express purpose of strengthening and renewing culture, inventing it and making it new as well as drawing on old stories. Massacres and brutality feature in his art but you would never know they were there without the titles. In these works, history is shown to be a receptive space as wide as the land where it spreads its implications and its repercussions. Thomas's paintings often have large patchy streaky surfaces of gritty, textured ground ochres mixed with tree gum. They show the artist's working gestures, as well as implying vast emotional spaces and the abstract malleable texture of thought and memory.

The tradition of painting Rover started at Warmun blossomed in the work of many artists, including Hector Jandany, a man of great charisma and warmth whom I met briefly in Darwin at an exhibition opening. Jandany and George Mung Mung helped set up a bicultural Gija/Christian school in the seventies called the Bough Shed School, and Jandany's paintings, which often brought together Christian and Gija imagery, were used for teaching. Jandany's technique was to underpaint with thin gritty ochre paint then scrape back the surface with a smooth flat stone before applying more layers of thin paint. He said he got this technique from his grandfather, who used to smooth rockfaces with a stone before painting on them. In their soft ochre colours and delicate forms of trees and hills, bodies of land and of water painted from memory, Jandany's works possess great emotional resonance, like fragile dreams.

Another Aboriginal artist who brought together Western and Aboriginal stories was Lin Onus, who was born in Melbourne in 1948 to a Scottish mother and Wiradjuri father. His father Bill Onus was famous for his land rights activism, as well as his business, Aboriginal Enterprise Novelties, which produced boomerangs, woomeras, fabrics and greeting cards imprinted with Aboriginal motifs. Lin learned to paint there and later at a panelbeater's shop. In 1986 he was invited to travel to Maningrida in Arnhem Land, became a member of the Wunuwun family there and then made annual visits. He said that the most valuable thing he learned from the famous artist and second father to him,

Jack Wunuwun, was to approach life with a sense of humour. His paintings often combined detailed photographic realism with *rarrk* patterning, traditional cross-hatching used to give the 'singing' power of iridescence (which is also ancestral power) to painted surfaces in Arnhem Land.

One of Onus's most famous works called *Fruitbats* (1991) uses a Hills Hoist clothesline as a roost for bats, which are painted with *rarrk* crosshatch patterns. The Hills Hoist clothesline is a South Australian invention of a single metal pole with four metal ribs spreading from the centre. Between the ribs is wire on which the clothes are pegged. The real genius of the Hills Hoist is the winding mechanism that allows the frame to be raised and lowered and thus to spin in the wind. Its inventor Lance Hill wanted 'Mum' to be able to get all those clothes hung up from one place, and not have to be walking all along the clothesline. Onus's *Fruitbats* combines this striking and now ordinary though slightly endangered Australian invention with roosting bats. Beneath his Hills Hoist lie scattered flowers. These decorative star patterns appear to have slid off the skins of the bats and lie on the ground like the spattered residue of the bats' faeces, demonstrating the convergence of beauty and the mundane, decoration and meaning.

In 1986 I stayed for two weeks on Aboriginal land at Ernabella where a friend was working as a teacher, though my permit to be there didn't arrive until after my return. When I arrived any Aboriginal person I was introduced to immediately called me *kunmanara*, and I found out that someone with a name like mine had recently died so I was called *kunmanara*, a name that fills in for anyone with a name the same as or similar to that of the recently deceased so that the dead person's name is not spoken. So I felt a little like a ghost as I walked around the settlement and visited the art and craft centre, which was very quiet at the time though the air was dense with the smell of wax and dyes from the batik workshop. I wanted to buy a *punu*, a poker-worked wooden lizard, but no-one wanted to sell it to me. They told me to come back later or ask someone else about it.

While my friend was teaching I read and went for walks. I saw and heard many crows and saw a few dingoes, but they didn't come near me. Someone told me that one side of the Musgrave Ranges that ring the settlement of Ernabella are men's mountains so I knew not to walk there. Each day I climbed to the top of the ridge near my friend's house and after walking along it quite a way sat down and made small drawings of the horizon in blue, yellow and red pastels on small carefully torn sheets of paper attached to a piece of wood with crocodile clips. My goal was to draw the entire horizon, and I had to work solidly to get it done in the time I had. I went to the same vantage point on the ridge every day and looked at the horizon to find the place where I had left off the previous day. It meant becoming familiar with where I was to the extent of giving names to the mountains and valleys, names like soft three leaning, lumpy edge, flat blue or red behind steep blue. This type of drawing is like touching something a long way away with your eyes and transferring that touch to something you can sense in your hands.

One day as I walked back to the settlement some young Aboriginal men called out to me to ask if I had found any gold. My friend informed me that this was a joke about the fabled Lasseter's Reef, a legendary gold deposit first 'found' in 1897. Among the prints that I made from my drawings back in Canberra were twelve black and white woodcuts that I called *Pitjatjanjara country – the ladder* because I thought about climbing the hills and about what Margaret Preston had said about the ladder of art, and because the landscape seemed to me somehow endlessly revolving and circular. Though there were twelve prints hung on the wall they were six images printed twice which joined each other to emphasise a dreamlike sense of containment, recurrence and circularity.

Another country was the title I gave to a set of colour reduction linocut prints that I made from my drawings of the horizon. The space between where I lived in Canberra and Ernabella was so wide. Being in Ernabella was like being in another country with its own rules and language. I was a foreigner there, yet the prints I made in response to that place are vibrant and loving, full of energy and colour, movement and light. In no small way they resemble works by Aboriginal artists made in the last twenty years suggesting that the colour, the energy and mystery, the knowledge in the land, can be discerned without being taught it or indeed quite knowing what it is, or indeed that the land speaks through art.

I called another set of linocuts, a whole wall of repeated colours and shapes, valleys and hills, *Ngura Palya Pulka* meaning 'Our Country/Camp/Home, Good, Beautiful' in Pitjantjatjara. I walked down the hill from the art school to the Institute of Aboriginal and Torres Strait Islander Studies to ask for the translation for this title and they phoned Ernabella to check with someone there. I found the Central Australian country to be exquisitely beautiful and was thinking of Gauguin's *Nave Nave Fenua*, which I understood to be Tahitian for *Beautiful Beautiful Land*, which is what I wanted translated into the local language. The Institute told me there was no direct translation for the words 'land' or 'beautiful'.

Perhaps Canberra, heart country to me, a place quite unreal with its art deco buildings perched around its artificial lake, its close embrace by twenty-one hills, its long views of the blue mountains of the Brindabella mountain range, its proximity to the whispering bush, and the frequent possibility, when you go for a walk to a hill on the edge of a suburb, of surprising a kangaroo lying in the shade, does have some connection to Central Australia; perhaps it is the light, the clear air and the far horizons.

The tendency of cultures to incorporate new things, to adapt and to find a place for strangers and strangeness, to connect the new with the old, is a significant part of art's invention, richness and purpose, as it means there is no other, no outsider, nothing that can not be somehow included or accounted for in the world.

Homology means the drawing of correspondences, the recognition of sameness between things. It could involve the indication of likeness, the locating of metaphors, similes, analogies between landforms and the human body. It can be an ecological way of thinking, to talk about relationships between things, the layering of meanings emphasising connections and interdependence. Seeing the earth as a body and the human body as like the earth develops a sense of connection as well as affection. This is not an intellectual affinity – the place of emotion is primary. Anthropologist Sylvie Poirier in writing about her fieldwork in Balgo in the Great Sandy Desert emphasises the Kutjungka people's sense of interconnectedness with and relatedness to the world:

> *Going through the land with Aboriginal people, nothing remains unexplained: each mark, each stone, each tree, must contain meaning which the Tjukurrpa (the Law, the Dreaming) has bequeathed to them ... In the Western Desert nothing is taken at face value, the meaning of everything is investigated: a solitary cloud, the song of a bird, a falling star, a birthmark, a sickness, a stone.*

Such reading of the world as a book is one way of finding a place in it.

December

The dog and I sit very still in the summer heat. Well actually I sit and he lies, close by, legs straight out, eyes closed, soaking up the heat until he can't possibly take any more, is panting hard and has to sit in the shade for a while, but always keeping a close eye and ear on me. I have a hat and long-sleeved shirt on and am folded over against the sun but want to be heated by that radiant heat that is like no other. If I sit still for long enough I know I will see or hear something; a camouflaged moth folded flat and symmetrical on a piece of wood, the bright yellow lumps of pollen on the back legs of a bee, a dead beetle being taken apart by ants, a spider repairing its web; I will see a breath of the wind move through the leaves; I might pat the trunk of a tree or run my finger over the sharp spikes of the quartz crystals hidden in some of the rocks edging our garden. When I was a child the pathways outside this house were covered in crushed quartz rock from the nearby quarry. I would walk up the hill with the sun behind me in order to spot the gleam where the face of a crystal was catching the sun and then walk towards that light to pick it up.

References

EPIGRAPHS

General
Oleg Grabar, *The Mediation of Ornament*, Princeton University Press, 1992, page 227.

January
Zbigniew Herbert, 'Pebble' in *Zbigniew Herbert: Selected Poems* (trans. Czeslaw Milosz & Peter Dale Scott), Penguin, 1968, page 108.

February
Judith Wright, 'The World and the Child', in *Mainly Modern: an anthology of verse selected by John and Dorothy Colmer*, Rigby, 1969, page 206.

March
Ticio Escobar, 'Identity and Myth Today', in *The Third Text Reader on Art, Culture and Theory*, (eds) Rasheed Araeen, Sean Cubitt, Ziauddin Sardar, Continuum, 2002, page 151.

April
Toss Woolaston, 'Man's Predicament in his Own World', *Christchurch Star*, 14 October 1959 (review of the Elias paintings); quoted in 'Chronology', Marja Bloem and Martin Browne, *Colin McCahon: A Question of Faith*, Craig Poton Publishing/Stedelijk Museum Amsterdam, 2004, page 192.

May
Gulumbu Yunupingu, at her November 2004 exhibition *Garak, the Universe* at Alcaston Gallery, reported by Patrick Hutchings, *The Age*, 14 January 2006.

June

Albrecht Dürer, *Painters' Manual*, quoted in J.C. Hutchison, *Albrecht Dürer: A Biography*, Princeton University Press, 1990, page 68.

July

Virginia Woolf, *Three Guineas*, (first published 1938), Blackwell, 2001, page 99.

August

Djon Mundine, 'Ich bin ein Aratjara', *Art Monthly Australia*, no. 75, 1994, pages 10–11.

September

Franz Fanon, *Black Skin, White Masks*, Pluto, page 229, as quoted in Homi K. Bhabha, *The Location of Culture*, Routledge, 1994, page 8.

October

John Ruskin *The Laws of Fésole*, (first published 1879), Allworth Press, 1996, page 39.

November

Agnes Martin, *Writings*, (ed.) Dieter Schwarz, 1991, Cantz Verlag, Germany, page 16, published to accompany exhibition *Agnes Martin: paintings and works on paper*, 1960–1989, Kunstmuseum Winterthur, 19 January – 15 March, 1992.

December

Trinh T. Minh-ha, installation with Jean-Paul Bourdier, *The Other Walk*, Musée du Quai Branly, Paris, 2006–2009, noted June 2007, Paris.

References

QUOTES IN TEXT

PAGE viii
Gillian Perry, *Paula Modersohn-Becker: Her Life and Work*, (diary entry by Modersohn-Becker), The Women's Press, 1979, page 26.

PAGE 1
Constantine P. Cavafy, 'Waiting for the Barbarians' (1904), in *Collected Poems* (translated by Edmund Kelley & Philip Sherrard), Princeton University Press, 1975, revised 1992.

PAGE 1
John Clark, *Modern Asian Art*, Craftsman House, 1998, page 9.

PAGE 2
Anselm Kiefer in *Boundaries, tracks, traces, songs: Anselm Kiefer in Australia*, Art and Australia supplement, Volume 30, Number 2, Fine Arts Press, 1992, page 11.

PAGES 6–7
Marcia Langton, 'Whitefella Jump Up' Correspondence, *Quarterly Essay*, Issue 12, 2003, Black Inc, page 80.

PAGE 31
Rhys Jones, quoted in Graeme Leech, 'The first boat people', *The Australian Magazine*, 18–19 July, 1998, page 21.

PAGE 38
Murray, Les, 'The Human-hair thread', *Meanjin*, vol. 38, no. 4, December, 1977, pages 550–571.

PAGE 39
Jill Kerr Conway, *The Road From Coorain*, (first published 1989), Minerva, 1994, page 25.

AN OPENING

PAGE 39

Randolph Stow, 'Raw Material', (first published in 1961), reprinted in Leonie Kramer and Adrian Mitchell (eds) *The Oxford Anthology of Australian Literature*, Melbourne, Oxford University Press, 1985, page 314.

PAGE 39

Heinrich von Kleist in *Caspar David Friedrich 1774–1840*, (eds) William Vaughan, Helmut Borsch-Supan, Hans Joachim Neidhardt, The Tate Gallery, 1972, page 107.

PAGE 47

Judith Ryan, 'Rarrk on bark: John Mawurndjul's medium of power and beauty', *Between Indigenous Australia and Europe: John Mawurndjul*, (eds) Claus Volkenandt & Christian Kaufmann, Aboriginal Studies Press, 2009, page 69.

PAGE 49

Rhys Jones, 'Ordering the Landscape', in (eds) Ian and Tamsin Donaldson, *Seeing the First Australians*, Unwin Hyman, Sydney, 1985, page 1985, reproduced in *Edge of the Trees*, (ed.) Dinah Dysart, Historic Houses Trust of New South Wales, 2000, page 6.

PAGE 61

Erwin Panofsky, *The Life and Art of Albrecht Dürer*, 1945, Princeton University Press, page 283.

PAGE 66

Sigmund Freud, *Civilisation and Its Discontents*, (first published 1930), The International Psycho-Analytical Library, (ed.) John D. Sutherland, No. 17, translated by Joan Riviere, revised and edited by James Strachey, Hogarth Press, 1963, page 1.

PAGE 75

John Ruskin, *Works*, vii.52, (eds) E.T. Cook and A. Wedderburn, London, 1903–12, 39 vols., quoted by Bernard Smith, *European*

References

Vision and the South Pacific, (first published 1960), Oxford University Press, 1989, page 339.

PAGE 77

Instructions to Captain Cook, 30 July 1768.
www.foundingdocs.gov.au/resources/transcripts/nsw1_doc_1768.pdf

PAGE 78

Transcribed by author from Paddy Wainburranga in *Too Many Captain Cooks,* 1988, film produced and directed by Penny McDonald, 1989.

PAGES 78–79

Harry Wedge, *Adam and Eve getting evicted* 1992, acrylic on canvas board, 20.5 x 40.5 cm. Reproduced with text in H.J. Wedge, *Wiradjuri Spirit Man*, Craftsman House published in association with Boomalli Aboriginal Artists Co-operative, 1996, page 80.

PAGE 90

Peter Yates, Clive Scollay, Penny Tweedie, 'Aboriginal Artists from Arnhemland', *European Dialogue: Biennale of Sydney* 1979, Art Gallery of New South Wales, unpaginated.

PAGE 90–91

Ian Hughes, 'Yolgnu Rom: Indigenous Knowledge in North Australia', in *Indigenous Organisations and Development*, (eds) P. Blunt and D.M. Warren, Intermediate Technology.

PAGE 95

E.H. Gombrich, *The Story of Art*, (first published in 1950), Phaidon Press, 1970, page 32.

PAGE 96

Geoffrey Bardon and James Bardon, *Papunya: A Place made after the Story*, Miegunyah Press, 2004, page 42.

AN OPENING

PAGES 96–97

James Bardon, *Revolution by Night or Karkalla Warnun (The Son after the Father)*, Local Consumption, 1991, pages 226–240.

PAGE 99

W.E.H. Stanner, 'The Dreaming' (1953) in *White Man got no Dreaming: Essays 1938–1973*, Australian National University Press, 1979, page 24.

PAGE 99

Peter Sutton, *Dreamings: The Art of Aboriginal Australia*, 1988, Asia Society, South Australia Museum, page 13.

PAGE 99

Don Gumana, quoted in Djalu Gurruwiwi, 'The Gälpu Story', *The Painters of the Wagilag Sisters Story 1937–1997*, (eds) Wally Caruana and Nigel Lendon, National Gallery of Australia, 1997, page 130.

PAGE 101

Geoffrey Bardon, *Aboriginal Art of the Western Desert*, Rigby, 1979, page 12.

PAGE 119

Peter Sutton, 'Aboriginal art, the nation state, suburbia', *Artlink* Vol. 12, No. 3, Spring, 1992, page 8.

PAGES 119–120

Deborah Bird Rose with Sharon D'Amico, Nancy Daiyi, Kathy Deveraux, Margaret Daiyi, Linda Ford and April Bright, *Country of the Heart: an Indigenous Australian Homeland*, Institute of Aboriginal Studies Press, 2002, page 15.

PAGE 120

Michael Mel, 'Art/Body: The Liminal Experiences of Indigeneity', *Artlink*, Vol. 20, No. 3, 2000, page 43.

References

PAGES 120–121

Fiona Hall, artist's statement, February 2002, footnote to Jason Smith, 'Fiona Hall: Dead in the Water' in *Fieldwork: Australian Art 1968–2002*, National Gallery of Victoria, 2002, page 130.

PAGE 122

Fiona Hall, 'Cell culture', *2002 Adelaide Biennial of Australian Art, Converge: where art and science meet*, Art Gallery of South Australia, 2002, page 38.

PAGE 124

Beth Hatton, 'Balancing' in exhibition catalogue *Below the Surface: a contemporary textiles exhibition resulting from a collaborative curatorial process*, (ed.) Jennifer Lamb, Goulburn Regional Art Gallery, 1996, pages 33–34.

PAGE 126

Toni Morrison, 'The Site of Memory', in *Out There: Marginalization and Contemporary Culture*, (eds) Russell Ferguson, Martha Gever, Trinh T. Minh-ha, Cornel West, The MIT Press, page 305.

PAGE 129

Margaret Preston, 'From Eggs to Electrolux', (first published *Art and Australia*), 3rd Series, no. 22, December 1927; republished in Margaret Preston, *Art and Australia: selected writings 1920–1950*, (ed.) Elizabeth Butel, Richmond, 2003, page 24.

PAGE 135

Transcribed by author from video by Joy Hardman, *I Spy*, 1997.

PAGE 138

ngurra(camp/home/country): Dolly Nampijinpa and Anne Mosey, exhibition catalogue, University of South Australia Art Museum, 1994, pages 21–22.

AN OPENING

PAGE 139

Leah King-Smith, 'The Nineteenth Century Photographs in Patterns of Connection', *Art Monthly,* special supplement, 1993, page 41.

PAGE 140

Duncan King-Smith, 'Statement', *Leah King-Smith: Patterns of Connection*, Australian Centre for Photography, Sydney, 1992, page 8.

PAGE 144

Wystan Curnow, *Colin McCahon, Gates and Journeys*, Auckland City Art Gallery, 1988, page 54.

PAGE 144

Peter Hooper, 'Can you hear me St Francis?' title of IX section of poem in *Earth Marriage* 1972, reference in *Colin McCahon, Gates and Journeys*, Auckland City Art Gallery, 1988, page 93.

PAGE 152

Claude Lévi-Strauss, *Triste Tropiques*, (first published 1955) 1973, translated by John and Doreen Weightman, Jonathan Cape, pages 414–415.

PAGE 158

Sylvie Poirier, *Les Jardins des Nomade: Territoire, rêve et transformation dans les groupes Aborigenes de Desert Occidental Australien*, 1990, Quebec: PhD thesis, Laval University, page 66, translated and quoted by Christine Watson, *Piercing the Ground*, Fremantle Arts Centre Press, 2003, page 57.

Index

A
Leonard Adams 12
Albertina Museum 52
Alterrenge 97
American literal-mindedness 115
Anbarra people 90
ANU archaeology department 149
Arnhem Land 89, 151
Ashmolean Museum 33, 123
Asia-Pacific Triennial 105
Aurukun 86, 147
Australian Institute of Aboriginal Studies 90
Australian irreverence 115

B
Babakiueria 134
Geoffrey Bardon 95, 101
James Bardon 96
Roland Barthes, *Mythologies* 87
Rex Battarbee, *Modern Australian Aboriginal Art* 84
John Berger, *Ways of Seeing* 87
Ingmar Bergman 36
Biennale of Sydney 89, 90, 129, 136
Big Tom, *Sunwoman at Wurriyupi* 93
Bitumen River Gallery 129
Gerry Blitner 64
Hieronymous Bosch xi, 23, 122
Annemarie Brody (ed.) *The Face of the Centre* 81
Johnny Bulun Bulun 151

C
C.V. Cavafy 1
Bruce Chatwin 2
Canaletto 87
Canberra 86, 156
Canberra School of Art 88, 151
Cape York 86, 99, 148, 151
Celtic fatalism 115
Azaria Chamberlain 150
Chambers Gully 115

Chasm Island 66
Childers Street 87
John Clark 1
Jill Kerr Conway 39
Captain Cook 77
Coranderk, Ramahyuck,
   Lake Tyers 140
Andrew Crocker (ed.)
   *Mr Sandman Bring Me a
   Dream* 81
Wystan Curnow 144

D

Dragon Trees 24
Dreaming/s 76, 97
*Dreamings: The Art of
   Aboriginal Australia*
   exhibition 93
Marcel Duchamp, *Fountain*
   73
Albrecht Dürer 52
Jack Dutruc 96

E

East Berlin 70
East Prussia 109
Edge of the Trees 48
Peter Egerton-Warburton
   136
Emperor of Qin 106
Epam epama (nothing is
   nothing) 99

Ernabella 155
Ticio Escobar 23, 50

F

Henri Fantin-Latour 10
Franz Fanon 103
Matthew Flinders 64
Sigmund Freud, *Civilisation
   and its Discontents* 66
Caspar David Friedrich 36
Furry Freak Brothers 149

G

Paul Gauguin 157
Elizabeth Gertsakis 111
Frank Gillen 97
E.H. Gombrich 95
Groote Eylandt 62, 84
Don Gumana 99

H

Basil Hall 151
Fiona Hall 120
Joy Hardman 134
Beth Hatton 123
Zbigniew Herbert 10
Werner Herzog 27
Lance Hill, Hill's Hoist
   155
Hiroshige 17
Dustin Hoffman 5
Peter Hooper 144

Index

I
Institute of Anatomy, Canberra 86, 147
Institute of Modern Art, Brisbane 136
Irish tongue 115

J
Hector Jandany 154
Tove Jansson 149
Jewish chutzpah 115
Jewish question 118
Vivien Johnson 7, 100
Rhys Jones 141

K
kanamb 120
Immanuel Kant 109
Matire Kereama, *The Lark's Song* 144
Anselm Kiefer 1, 124
Martin King 151
Leah King-Smith 139
Paul Klee xi
Emily Kame Kngwarreye 43, and her dog 82
Käthe Kollwitz 109
Königsberg 109
kunmanara 155
Karel Kupka 62
Akira Kurosaki 150

L
Lajamanu 90
Marcia Langton 6, 88
Lasseter's Reef 156
D.H. Lawrence 109
Claude Lévi-Strauss, *Triste Tropiques* 152

M
MacDonnell Ranges 85
Ludwig Hirschfeld Mack 12
Bea Maddock 140
Mallee 111
Maningrida 154
Gillian Mann 71
Banduk Marika 151
Wandjuk Marika 43
Agnes Martin 128
Maud 149
Colin McCahon 128–132
Frederick McCarthy 86, 148
Ellen McIlwaine 88
Megalo International Silkscreen Collective Workshop 44
Michael Mel 120
Herman Melville 87
Melville Island 93
Michael Perry Reserve 101

Michelangelo 106
Bette Mifsud 108
Mildura Palimpsest 124
Alex Miller 118
Trinh T. Minh-ha 147
Missionaries, misfits and mercenaries 135
Paula Modersohn-Becker x
Moomintrolls 149
Toni Morrison 126
Anne Mosey 136
Mount Liebig 93
Djon Mundine 81
Les Murray 38
Musgrave Ranges 156

N
Albert Namatjira 85
Dolly Nampitjinpa 136
National Film and Sound Archive 86
National Gallery of Australia 62, 87, 91
National Gallery of Victoria 81
National Museum of Australia 65
Mr Natural 149
ngurra (camp / home / country) 136
Nuremberg 52

O
Oceania 66
Bill Onus 154
Lin Onus 154

P
Painters of the Western Desert: Clifford Possum, Uta Uta Tjangala, and Paddy Carroll Jungarai exhibition 92
Palm Valley 85
Papunya 99
Peter Peemuggina 99
Phar Lap 86
W.C. Piguenit 41
Pioneer Women's Trail 145
Sylvie Poirier 158
Jackson Pollock 82
Pompeii 70
Port Jackson Painter 27
Clifford Possum 7, 100
Powhatan Mantle 33, 123
Margaret Preston 129, 156
Thomas Pynchon 87

R
Alfred Radok 72
Rajah and Ranee 110
Ramingining 89

Index

Paloma Ramos 107
Reichskristallnacht 110
Rainer Maria Rilke 110
Rodin 106
Romain Roland 66
Rom ceremony 90
Deborah Bird Rose 119
Mark Rothko 82
John Ruskin 75, 116
Judith Ryan 47

S
Salvage anthropology 75
Schloss Hernstein 57
Second Creek 101
E.H. Shepard 149
Simone Martini 129
Simryn Gill 113
Skeeter 79
Bernard Smith, *European Vision and the South Pacific* 75
Grace Cossington Smith 19
St Francis of Assisi 37, 144
W.E.H. Stanner (Everywhen) 99
State Library of Victoria 139
Randolph Stow 39
Charles Sturt 96
Sturt's *Journal* 96
Peter Sutton 99, 119

T
Tandanya 78, 93
Tasmanian Aboriginal languages 143
Teddy 54
Telecom 99
Terra Australis Incognita 77
Teutonic gloom 115
The Aboriginal Memorial 47
Theresienstadt 110
Rover Thomas 82, 153
Tiananmen Square 105
Mick Wallangkarri Tjakamarra, *Old Man's Dreaming on Death or Destiny* 91
Tim Leura Tjapaltjarri 7, 100
Johnny Warangula Tjupurrula 91, 101
Turkey Tolson Tjupurrula 81, 93
Too Many Captain Cooks 77
Tower of Babel 114
Toyota Dreaming 100
Transit of Venus 77
Theo Tremblay 151
Truganini 142
Tony Tuckson 46
Jennifer Turpin and Michaelie Crawford 124
Tutini 45

V

Petronella Vaarzon-Morel 138
Vincent van Gogh xi, 21
Vegemite 69
Venice 70

W

Paddy Fordham Wainburrunga 77
Andy Warhol 73
Warlpiri 90, 98, 153
Warmun (Turkey Creek) 153
Waterfall Gully Road 115
Harry Wedge, *Adam and Eve getting evicted* 78
William Westall 64
Western Desert 82, 91, 95
Patrick White, *Voss* 87
Wik people 86, 148
Winnie the Pooh 149
Wititj 99
Toss Woolaston 36, 129
Virginia Woolf 62
World Council of Indigenous People's conference 32, 88, 91
Judith Wright 17
Jack Wunuwun 151, 155

X

Ah Xian 103

Y

Yirrkala 151
Yuendumu 136
Yugoslavia 70
Yulara 150
Gulumbu Yunupingu 43

Z

Zippy the pinhead 149

Wakefield Press is an independent publishing and
distribution company based in Adelaide, South Australia.
We love good stories and publish beautiful books.
To see our full range of books, please visit our website at
www.wakefieldpress.com.au
where all titles are available for purchase.
To keep up with our latest releases, news and events,
subscribe to our monthly newsletter.

Find us!

Facebook: www.facebook.com/wakefield.press
Twitter: www.twitter.com/wakefieldpress
Instagram: www.instagram.com/wakefieldpress

www.ingramcontent.com/pod-product-compliance
Lightning Source LLC
Chambersburg PA
CBHW071023240526
45469CB00006BD/2068